BORN IN 1972?
WHAT ELSE HAPPENED?

PUBLISHED BY BOOM BOOKS
www.boombooks.biz

ABOUT THIS SERIES

.... But after that, I realised that I knew very little about these parents of mine. They had been born about the start of the Twentieth Century, and they died in 1970 and 1980. For their last 50 years, I was old enough to speak with a bit of sense.

I could have talked to them a lot about their lives. I could have found out about the times they lived in. But I did not. I know almost nothing about them really. Their courtship? Working in the pits? The Lock-out in the Depression? Losing their second child? Being dusted as a miner? The shootings at Rothbury? My uncles killed in the War? Love on the dole? There were hundreds, thousands of questions that I would now like to ask them. But, alas, I can't. It's too late.

Thus, prompted by my guilt, I resolved to write these books. They describe happenings that affected people, real people. The whole series is, to coin a modern phrase, designed to push your buttons, to make you remember and wonder at things forgotten.

The books might just let nostalgia see the light of day, so that oldies and youngies will talk about the past and re-discover a heritage otherwise forgotten. Hopefully, they will spark discussions between generations, and foster the asking and answering of questions that should not remain unanswered.

BORN IN 1972?

WHAT ELSE HAPPENED?

RON WILLIAMS

AUSTRALIAN SOCIAL HISTORY

BOOK 34 IN A SERIES OF 35 FROM 1939 to 1973

War Babies Years (1939 to 1945):   7 Titles
Baby Boom Years (1946 to 1960):   15 Titles
Post Boom Years (1961 to 1972):   13 Titles

BOOM, BOOM BABY, BOOM

BORN IN 1972? WHAT ELSE HAPPENED?

Published by Boom Books
Wickham, NSW, Australia

Web: www.boombooks.biz
Email: jen@boombooks.biz

Creator: Williams, Ron, 1934- author.

Title: Born in 1972? What else happened?

ISBN: 9780645182620

Subjects: Australia, History, Miscellanea--20th Century.

Some Letters used in this text may still be in copyright. Every reasonable effort has been made to locate the writers. If any persons or ;their estates can establish authorship, and want to discuss copyright, please contact the author at:

jen@boombooks.biz

Cover images: National Archives of Australia:
M155 7530507 Prime Minister Whitlam in China
B941 5980698 Beach scene
J2364 31946541 Phone exchange old and new
B941 5984308 Child car safety seat

TABLE OF CONTENTS

SOME IMPORTANT PEOPLE AND EVENTS

Queen of Britain	Elizabeth II
PM of Oz, till Dec 2nd	W McMahon
PM of Oz, after Dec 2nd	Gough Whitlam
Opposit'n Leader, till Dec 2nd	Gough Whitlam
Governor General	Paul Hasluck
The Pope	Paul VI
US President	Richard Nixon
PM of Britain	Edward Heath

WINNER OF ASHES

1970/71	England 2 - 0
1972	Draw 2 - 2
1974 - 5	Australia 4 - 1

MELBOURNE OF MELBOURNE CUP

1971	Silver Knight
1972	Flying Lane
1973	Gala Supreme

ACADEMY AWARDS, 1972

Best Actor	Gene Hackman
Best Actress	Jane Fonda
Best Movie	French Connection

INTRODUCTION TO THIS SERIES

This book is the 34th in **a series of books** that I have researched and written. It tells a story about a number of important or newsworthy Australia-centric events that happened in 1972. The series covers each of the 35 years from 1939 to 1973 for a total of 35 books.

I developed my interest in writing these books a few years ago at a time when my children entered their teens. My own teens started in 1947, and I started trying to remember what had happened to me then. I thought of the big events first, like Saturday afternoon at the pictures, and cricket in the back yard, and the wonderful fun of going to Maitland on the train for school each day. Then I recalled some of the not-so-good things. I was an altar boy, and that meant three or four Masses a week. I might have thought I loved God at that stage, but I really hated his Masses. And the schoolboy bullies, like Greg Favell, and the hapless Freddie Bevan. Yet, to compensate for these, there was always the beautiful, black headed, blue-sailor-suited June Browne, who I was allowed to worship from a distance.

I also thought about my parents. Most of the major events that I lived through came to mind readily. But after that, I realised that I really knew very little about these parents of mine. They had been born about the start of the Twentieth Century, and they died in 1970 and 1980. For their last 20 years, I was old enough to speak with a bit of sense. I could have talked to them a lot about their lives. I could have found out about the times they lived in.

But I did not. I know almost nothing about them really. Their courtship? Working in the pits? The Lock-out in the Depression? Losing their second child? Being dusted as a miner? The shootings at Rothbury? My uncles killed in the War? There were hundreds, thousands of questions that I would now like to ask them. But, alas, I can't. It's too late.

Thus, prompted by my guilt, I resolved to write these books. They describe happenings that affected people, real people. In **1972,** there is some coverage of international affairs, but a lot more on social events within Australia. This book, and the whole series is, to coin a modern phrase, designed to push the reader's buttons, to make you remember and wonder at things forgotten. The books might just let nostalgia see the light of day, so that oldies and youngies will talk about the past and re-discover a heritage otherwise forgotten. Hopefully, they will spark discussions between generations, and foster the asking and the answering of questions that should not remain unanswered.

The sources of my material. I was born in 1934, so that I can remember well a great deal of what went on around me from 1939 onwards. But of course, the bulk of this book's material came from research. That meant that I spent many hours in front of a computer reading electronic versions of newspapers, magazines, Hansard, Ministers' Press releases and the like. My task was to sift out, **day-by-day**, those stories and events that would be of interest to the most readers. Then I supplemented these with materials from books, broadcasts, memoirs, biographies, government reports and statistics. And I talked to old-timers, one-on-one, and in organised groups, and to Baby Boomers and post Baby Boomers about their recollections. People with stories to tell come out of the woodwork, and talk no end about the tragic and funny and commonplace events that have shaped their lives.

The presentation of each book. For each year, the end result is a collection of Chapters on many of the topics that concerned ordinary people in that year. I think I have covered most of the major issues that people then were interested in. On the other hand, in some cases I have dwelt a little on minor frivolous matters, perhaps to the detriment of more sober considerations. Still, in the long run, this makes the book more readable, and hopefully it will convey adequately the spirit of the times.

I have been **deliberately national in outlook**, so that readers elsewhere will feel comfortable that I am talking about matters that affected them personally. After all, housing shortages and strikes and juvenile delinquency involved **all** Australians, and other issues, such as problems overseas, had no State component in them.

Overall, I expect I can make you wonder, remember, rage and giggle equally, no matter where you hail from. Here though, in the short run, I will start by presenting some background material from the year **1971** that should get you started.

THE VIETNAM WAR

The major topic for conversations throughout 1971 was still the Vietnam War. This tragic upheaval, a war between America and China, had dragged on since before the mid-Sixties. It had forced most of the world into two armed camps who did whatever they could to kill each other.

The Americans were supposedly inspired by a hatred of Communism, and the fear that it would spread from China right through the Asia Pacific, down into Tasmania. The Chinese, in return, believed that America was Satan, and that it was surreptitiously colonising the region.

But both of these fears were only a cover-up for the fact that the philosophies of China and America were completely different and had been since before the Communist Reds consolidated their power in China in 1949. At the present time, each of them was trying to show the world that **it was bigger and better than the other**. One way of doing this was to have a spectacular fight, and each of them believed that a victory would somehow win it friends.

So they picked Vietnam as a site to fight. This was convenient because it meant that they were not fighting on their home turf. Also, North and South Vietnam were already at each other's throats, and almost at civil war, over such matters as the colonial Dutch leaving Vietnam, and ending their centuries of domination.

By 1972, the War was out of favour in most countries. In the US, support for continuing was well short of 50 per cent. This had dropped massively as various scandals erupted over the conduct of American troops in Vietnam. And as hope now faded of getting an easy victory.

In Australia, mothers and families just wanted their young men to come home. To them, why stay in a War where their menfolk could be killed just because of some silly theory about Chinese domination?

Granted, by now, we had officially stopped fighting, and most of our boys were on the way home. But many stragglers were still being killed. And there was always the fear that war might beak out again, and our boys, now veterans, **would be recalled to the fight**.

As more and more of the Australian population called for stopping the War, and as the Government continued withdrawing troops, our population here settled down. The demonstrations and punch-ups, that were common earlier, disappeared almost, and some of the population felt it was now possible to talk sensibly and quietly about the terrible cost of the War on the nation, and on the dead men and their families.

CHINA OUT OF THE DOG HOUSE

The War was still going ahead in Vietnam, with hundreds on both sides being killed every day. But, curiously, behind the scenes, there were some hints that both sides were utterly tired of its futility and were prepared to stop the fighting.

One major indication of this was that at the end of 1971, the USA removed its veto on China joining the United Nations as a member state. Up till now, China was a pariah, and would never be allowed in. Now, here it was, with full veto powers itself.

So maybe, just maybe, this bonhomie **might** extend outside the bureaucrats in Washington, even to the killing fields in Vietnam.

SEAT BELTS IN CARS

In NSW, and the other States at different times, **seat belts in cars and other vehicles were made mandatory.** At first, this applied to the drivers only, but gradually passengers were added to the list.

There were many drivers in the nation who refused to wear them, and for a decade there were constant battles between the Police and these. Gradually though, the good sense of the measure was proven by the results, and the exceptional rebel has just about disappeared. This took only 50 years.

SMOKE GETS IN YOUR LUNGS

Prior to WWII, more than half the population of men enjoyed some form of smoking. Pipes were popular with the older men. With the younger brigade, there were many who rolled their own, with processed tobacco, and some form of rice paper. Though again, there were a few who wrapped their tobacco in used newspapers. Cigars were never popular in Australia.

Only a few were able to afford proper **cigarettes**, imported from America, with all the sleek packaging and smooth promoting that our American friends enjoyed.

With the advent of the War, Australian men in uniform were **given a ration of cigarettes**, and the popularity of this form of smoking quickly replaced other forms. By the end of the War, smoking these had become very popular, and few men could function without a packet of gaspers every day.

Women were not to be left out of the act. During the War, once again it became a mark of sophistication for women of all ages to have their puff throughout the day. Mind you, many of these felt shy about their vice, and hoped their mother would not find out.

But over the years, the stigma of women smoking slowly went. By 1972, over half the population huffed and puffed, indoors and outdoors, in trains, during theatre, in bars, at home, in other peoples' homes, and sometimes in churches.

In the background, there was a substantial amount of serious research that was pointing out the connection between smoking and various forms of lung disease. But in Oz, at this time, no one was going to spoil the party. In fact, the party here was just beginning, and consumption of the weed grew yearly.

Over the next decades the battle continued and by now, as you well know, the pendulum has swung against tobacco products. It is worthwhile, however, to consider how society will fare if some form of marijuana is legalised in Australia as it has been in much of the world.

I suggest that again the battle will be just as fierce, and might again last another 50 years.

NOTES FOR READERS

FIRST NOTE. Throughout this book, I rely a lot on reproducing **Letters** from the newspapers. Whenever I do this, I put the text in a different font, and indent it a little, and make the font somewhat smaller. **I do not edit the text at all**. That is, I do not correct spelling or grammar. If the text gets at all garbled, I do not change it. It's just as it was seen in the Papers of the day.

SECOND NOTE, The material for this book, when it comes from newspapers, is reported as it was seen at the time. **If** the benefit of hindsight over the years changes things, then I **might** record that in **Comments**. The info reported thus reflects matters **as they were seen in 1972.**

THIRD NOTE. **Let me also apologise in advance to anyone I might offend**. In a work such as this, it is certain some people will think I got some things wrong. I am sure that I did, but please remember, all of this is **only my opinion**. And really, **my opinion does not matter one little bit in the scheme of things. I hope you will say "silly old bugger", and shrug your shoulders and keep reading on.**

So, now, 1972, here we come.

JANUARY NEWS ITEMS

Queen Elizabeth II started the New Year with her list of Honours. Hundreds of awards were granted across what was left of the Empire, but the main Australian interest was in the knighthoods....

Nineteen locals were appointed Knights. Many of these you have not heard of, but three were well known to everyone....

These were singer Joan Hammond, the Jockey George Moore, and tennis champion Evonne Goolagong. Others honoured were Robert Askin, Premier of NSW, and the Prime Minister, William McMahon....

The well-known French singer and dancer, **Maurice Chevalier, died aged 83**. Through his movies and live shows, he had entertained the world for half a century.

Two motorists collided in the middle of Melbourne city. **Both drivers got out quickly and ran off** in different directions. When the Police caught them, they found out that **both cars had been stolen**, and that the drivers were not keen on filling out Police Accident Reports.

An observer on a beach watched as **a turtle** climbed up the beach, dug a hole, laid over 100 eggs, covered the hole, and swam off. Nothing odd about this....

What was odd was that **the beach was at Merewether**, on the middle of the NSW coast. That is about 2,000 miles from the southern most point of the Great Barrier Reef. **Seems like someone took a wrong turn.**

In 1972, **Jack Mundy,** and associated **building unions,** bullied his way to prominence in the Sydney and Melbourne scenes by calling strikes that upset large scale development of properties....

While he horrified most of the population by his tactics, including calling strikes and associated punch-ups, he did give **the embryonic Green Movement a boost....**

The **environment cause** in the 1970's grew from backyard complainers on local issues, towards **the huge force that it is today.**

Shane Gould continued her winning ways by breaking the Women's freestyle world swimming record.

Another **world record fell to Australian** Bill Flewllyn of Adelaide when he stayed aloft in a kite for over 15 hours. The previous world record was about 12 hours.

The Singapore Government is cracking down on "long-haired gits" who want to enter their country....

One Australian was allowed to enter when he guaranteed to return to the Police with his hair cut. Others were rejected because of "their scruffy appearance".

In Dunedin, New Zealand, **a man** pleaded guilty to **"improperly interfering with human remains"....**

Previously, a NZ Cabinet Minister had committed suicide, and his body was laid to rest in a public cemetery. Some other person **raided the grave and took his skull,** and later **polished it thoroughly** and gave it to the accused. It was easily recognised by the gunshot wound to the forehead....

AN INSULAR JANUARY 1st

I looked round the newspapers on New Years Day for signs of what we might expect for the coming year. What did I find?

The Editor of the Sydney Morning Herald (*SMH*) gave a summary of what he saw as **international** prospects. This made dreary reading. He talked about Chinese-Russian rivalry, and Washington-Moscow polarisation. He was cautious about the Indo-Russian Treaty and the dangers it presented to the very future of Pakistan. He yet again warned us that the Middle East would still be a problem. He warned us that Australia, now hopefully emerging from the Vietnam War, should not relax in this "fluid opportunistic world".

Ho hum. We have heard all this a million times. This type of talk mattered not one little bit to Australians at this time. The nation was on holiday. People had flocked to the cities, or to the country, and were ready to watch tennis and cricket on the tellie, to play Chinese Checkers, and have a barbie every day. One glorious month ahead, with no newspapers and no calamities, and who cares if the Chinese or the Russians even exist.

Letters to the Editor showed the same indifference. There were only five Letters. The first was a reply to an earlier Editorial that talked about the Geneva Convention. The second talked about cars overtaking on the inside, and the third about poor seating at a concert. Then there was an attack on Gough Whitlam. The last one raised the burning issue of one-man rail cars.

In all, it was the typical start-of-the-Year welcome to another year. We, as a nation, were never much interested in matters far from our shores. We never worried too much about overseas all-consuming crisis.

We **did** get worried about big issues such as the Vietnam War, because it affected the lives and deaths of our men-folk. But our restraint, our general lack of concern, deliberately reflected our satisfaction with the idea that while we might not be quite up to date in worldly affairs, we liked it that way. We simply said let the rest of the world go by, **and often it did.**

AUSTRALIAN PARTY POLITICS

The Liberal Party was still in power in Canberra. It had held that position for about 20 years, and had held firm with the added help of a smaller Country Party.

But it was now in a difficult situation with its leadership. Menzies retired in 1966, Holt drowned in 1967. A stand-in McEwan lasted only three weeks. Reluctant John Gorton self-purged in just over two years. Now, an unpopular Billy McMahon was hanging on to Liberal leadership by avoiding any policy initiatives. That is, five leaders in less that six years. No political party enjoys that happening.

To make matters worse for them, Labor under Gough Whitlam was full of vigour and drive. Whitlam was a barrister, with great rhetorical skills, and a myriad of well-thought-out ideas that would change the nation. He cut the power of Labor's "36 Faceless Men" who had made policy decisions in the back-room for decades, and had thus opened up the Party to new policies that really might invigorate the nation.

By January 1972, it was certain that there would be a Federal election some time during the year, so we will watch with great interest an events unfold.

US, CHINESE BECOMING MATEY?

For a month or so, the corridors of Washington have heard wild talk that President Nixon would soon visit China.

Most people at first thought that this was nonsense. After all, the two nations in Vietnam were dropping bombs and napalm on each other, and were having hand-to-hand fights with each other, and proclaiming how right **their** cause was and what horrible monsters **the other party** was.

But now, early in January, it is slowly emerging that Nixon might indeed visit China, as early as February. If that did happen, it might mean the end of the War. Could this really happen? Could America pull out and still save face? After all their bluster and high principles? The two nations have held so called peace-talks for five years now, and have never even got close to a settlement. Could they somehow do it now?

We will have to hold our breath.

LOCAL POLLUTION

Early in the Seventies, Australia started to take up arms against all sorts of polluters. Much offence came from power stations, hospitals and factories which all had large towers to release their plumes of smoke. Another source was motor vehicles, and also planes. Again, **noise** pollution was attracting attention, coming from cars, motor bikes, and music venues and devices. This was a time when all of these irritations, that had long been accepted, started being resented and somehow fought against.

Another source of annoyance to common folk was the dumping of rubbish anywhere out of sight. The Letter below will remind readers of the good old days.

Letters, J Penney. It has become very obvious to me that the so-called anti-pollution campaign is a complete farce. From here to Wisemans Ferry has become one vast dumping ground for household garbage and any other rubbish deposited by passing motorists, without the slightest fear of retribution.

To give an illustration I telephoned Hornsby Council yesterday morning and informed them that a large quantity of filth crawling with maggots, together with cartons, beer bottles, etc, had been found outside my fence the previous evening, December 28, and that among it was an enevelope with a name and address and also a dry-cleaning ticket in the same name. Were they prepared to prosecute?

The following was their reaction: (1) "Did you see it dumped? (2) Can you prove that the name and address you hold is that of the offender?" (3) No, council would not prosecute. However, following my pressing request, a council officer arrived, took the name and address given, stated that council would probably write thereto, and that he would arrange removal of the rubbish.

No garbage service is provided by council in this area and when rubbish is taken to the nearest tip by the residents, it is subjected to an inspection, no "putrescible matter" being allowed in this sanctuary. Apparently the roadside is available for that.

I am required by law to prevent fruit fly on my property, local authority demands that water deposited on my roof by divine power is retained on my property, rates have to be paid for unlit, unsewered and unsealed roads, freely made available to the depredations of non-residents.

I might add that I rang the Department of Health (Division of Occupational Health and Pollution Control) for about 15 minutes on the same morning, but my calls were unanswered.

At 2pm today, December 30, the rubbish referred to had not been removed.

Comment. This was a problem all round Australia. One big source of this pollution was that local Councils seemed oblivious to it. There were no public bins, no Council cleanups, no fines for deviants, no control over dump sites or policing those persons littering.

Visitors to Australia often wrote to the newspapers saying what an ideal environment we had. But they remarked at how indifferent we were to the piles of rubbish and mess we accumulated.

In passing, I am happy to say that, 50 years later, we have got a lot better.

Second comment. It is worth noting that antagonism to all forms of environmental sinning was growing. Local Letters like the one above were stirring many pots. But importantly, such Letters were increasingly moving from the local area on to protests from organised groups and Associations.

A national voice against pollution was being heard for the first time. So much so that, fifty years later, it is often claimed that **environmental protections** are delaying and stifling developments.

We will see more of this pendulum starting to swing throughout this book.

NOT EVERYONE AGREES

When it comes to local noise, not everyone agrees.

Letters, W Fenn. The letter from Mrs Stubbs on backyard swimming pools makes me ponder on the rights of an individual to pursue a chosen activity within the confines of a home.

We consider ourselves very fortunate in having a backyard swimming pool, which is currently giving a great deal of pleasure to a number of neighbourhood children.

However, I am all in favour of councils looking into these matters, and suggest that consideration also be given to legislating on:

* Foolproof mufflers for lawnmowers.

* No laughter or audible signs of enjoyment after 9pm.

* A ban on electric shavers, food mixers, vacuum cleaners and all home power-tools between sunset and sunrise.

* The establishment of a "sound patrol" and security force to detect offenders.

Who knows? A new Solomon might emerge from the whole business. And, more importantly, it would distract our aldermen from such sordid matters as rate increases.

SCHOOLING A WASTE FOR MANY

The Editor of the *SMH* reviewed a number of speeches given by High School principals over the last month. He formed the opinion that most of them were leaning towards the view that Years Five and Six were often wasted years, with reluctant children forced to attend, and were keeping the pupils away from more suitable pursuits.

He argued that underlying this approach was the status race which demanded that parents lost prestige if their children did not go to University. Also, it appeared that children without a university degree would never rise to the top in any later employment.

One Victorian headmaster went so far as to describe the senior classes as little better than concentration camps of unemployment,where grown men and women are treated like children and kept in tutelage long after they should have been allowed to commence their adult lives.

He concludes that "surely it is time to end the conspiracy of silence about parental snobbery, to admit that far more pupils must be weeded out at the end of their fourth year, and to direct them into satisfying and more socially useful fields".

The response to the Editorial was substantial. The most common was that expressed by Mr Crowley below.

Letters, D Crowley. It is most depressing, in an affluent society such as ours, to find a journal of your standing declaring that too many students are staying at school for too long. Surely, the more education we give our young people the better, and our system of recruitment into employment should take account of this. Otherwise, something is very wrong with our system of values.

We should also devote more than the present pittance in continuing education into adulthood.

Mr Crowley had other thoughts and expressed them in another Letter.

Letters, D Crowley. Your editorial "School malaise" is a depressing statement. It also insults a great many parents in this State by describing them, most unfairly, as snobs.

It is not at all snobbish, surely, to desire the highest possible income for one's children in a society where income so largely determines the kind of life one can lead.

Parents did not create the status race: they are caught up in it. It is not their fault that high incomes go with high status. Even our taxation system is weighted in favour of those on high incomes.

So long as there is a chance that young people can make it into a prestige occupation - and educators are not able to predict later performance with much accuracy - one cannot blame parents for keeping them at school.

Further, there must be many parents who feel that their children have not had sufficient general education at the end of their fourth year at high school. At that age, many students are only beginning to realise what the finer things in life can mean to them; two more years of schooling, even at some risk to their employment prospects, can tremendously enrich the rest of their lives.

Letters, C Oliver, Principal, Mount Austin High School. This way points the return only to Victorian ideas of an educated elite and a working class of uneducated others, a concept that cannot be accepted by any Australian with his roots in democracy and his beliefs in equality of educational opportunity.

MARY HAD A HEAP OF MUTTON

The next Letter was written in 1972. But most meat buyers would recognise that it could have been written fifty years later, and most readers would still nod their heads in agreement.

Letters, F Hughes. As an ex-sheep and cattle producer I would like to draw attention to the retail meat situation here, particularly in regard to mutton and lamb.

Similar conditions exist with the local mutton and lamb market. So-called lamb chops are blatantly advertised and displayed as lamb in many butchers' shops, and are obviously hogget - and often wethers or culled ewes. How they fool the public is beyond me, as the size of some of these chops would do justice to a ram!

Some housewives obviously think that the bigger the chop, the bigger the value. It would seem that there is an apparent gross misuse of the "lamb" branding irons at certain places.

While the Government is inquiring into the American complaints, this local injustice could be more closely policed as, goodness knows, the price of this so-called lamb, compared with the price of sheep in the country, is an utter farce. Some mighty profits are going somewhere - certainly not to the farmers.

Comment. I know that over the last 50 years, across all States, regulations have come and gone that address this problem. But without lasting effect, many claim.

KANGAROO PRESERVATION

Kangaroos in the nation are always under attack It can be said that they destroy fences in the country areas, they eat crops, and uproot fields of recently-planted grain, and serve no purpose to mankind.

On the other hand, they stand as the national symbol, are of great tourist value, provide a living for many people in the meat trade, and the fur industry.

Argument is always raging about whether we have too many of them, and whether we should cull them, or place a bounty on their hides. The pendulum is always swinging.

In 1972, in many circles there was a feeling that the cull had gone too far, and that it should cease. Preservation Societies were formed around the nation, they were vocal in fighting against the "extinction of our roos in 20 years". One such saviour went to print. I have given a few of his ideas below.

Letters, F Jones, Kangaroo Protection Committee. All kangaroo killing must be based on strict biological principles, as is done in other countries Culling should never exceed the number of young produced and reaching maturity each year.

Other shortcomings of the report are:

(a) No recommendations to end the brutality.

(b) The acceptance of illegal spotlight shooting.

(c) No weight limit restriction for conserving the essential breeding stock of kangaroos.

(d) No income tax concession has been recommended for landholders who are prepared to leave part of their properties in natural state to help to conserve wildlife.

(e) Recommendations that full-time and part-time shooters be allowed an annual kill quota and that graziers be issued with permits to cull excess populations and sell the meat and skins can seriously threaten the kangaroo because of difficulties in enforcing such regulations.

(f) Joey care centres have not been recommended.

Two vital questions remain unanswered - what is the critical level for harvesting kangaroo populations and what is needed to ensure the survival of individual species.

Nature's unique breeding device for ensuring the survival of Big Red in the harsh inland is being brutally destroyed. When breeding females of this species are shot this can result in the destruction of four kangaroos - the mother, the dependent young-at-foot (which is unable to fend for itself), the pouch young and the dormant embryo. Statistics record the death of one kangaroo. Shooting and drought can eliminate the Red Kangaroo.

Let us be realistic, the existing kangaroo situation remains unchanged, the callous killing will continue while all Australians wait for a proper solution to be found before it is too late.

Live kangaroos are a tourist attraction - they are worth money! Tourism can earn more dollars for this country than many of our other industries.

We did our best to eliminate the koala, perhaps we can do better with the kangaroo.

Comment. Whether this type of agitation was successful in changing any opinions, I do not know. Nor do I know whether it affected any actions.

But what is obvious is that the roos are still surviving quite well in the outback of this nation, and their demise is not imminent.

MY JANUARY SELF-INDULGENCE

In writing these books, I occasionally get away from the news items that form the bulk of my copy, and just let my mind wander over a topic. I have no axes to grind, no fights to fight, but enjoy thinking back and forth over something that attracts my interest for half an hour. I am at that stage right now.

What started me off was the little Letter below that talks about vandalism in church graveyards and cemetries.

Letters, A Davis. I refer to the care and maintenance of that sacred piece of land known as the Randwick general cemetery.

We are among the fortunate ones whose family grave has not been desecrated; but the vandalism to some of the monuments, even those of recent origin, and extremely expensive memorials, is unbelievable as well as heartbreaking.

Surely Randwick Council, if this comes under its jurisdiction, could afford to erect, say, a barbed wire protection on the boundaries (not such a huge area), as is done by the armed services, or such, for the protection of their property.

I am sure it would be much cheaper than the money they have to outlay repairing the destruction to the toilets there, which are an utter disgrace.

It led me to question whether or not such behaviours increased in the fifty years since the Letter was written. My answer to that question was I think it has remained about the same. There is still the occasional report today about such desecration, even in the biggest establishment, and my memory suggests that the rate has been steady over the years.

This led me to a more interesting question of how funeral practices had varied in that period. **My earliest memory of funerals** was at about the age of ten years in my home town, Abermain, in the centre of the Cessnock coalfields. None of the impoverished miners had cars, and in any case, there was virtually no petrol.

But there **were** plenty of deaths from "falls in the pits." Dozens of men were killed each year, and the next afternoon most able-bodied persons walked for five miles, behind the coffin on a horse-drawn cart, to the nearest cemetery in a grim and solemn procession. **The body was buried**, and the 200 mourners walked home, still in gloom.

By the 1970's, the funeral industry was becoming aware of marketing, but was just learning its way in this. Bodies were now carried in coffins in hearses, most funerals were in churches with a few floral tributes, the mourners by now could all find a car to travel in. The funeral itself could only travel at 15 miles per hour, so traffic was blocked for the procession. After the burial, mourners again got into cars, and many of them went to the pub to celebrate the deceased's life.

Fifty years later, it is easy to find big changes. The body now is prepared for the funeral, all prettied up. It is put into a flash coffin, at a time when only the best is good enough. The body sometimes lies in state, perhaps for a week or more,with attendees invited to have a last look.

Women in white hats and suits, and men in black suits, flutter round, and attend to all perceived needs. The main events of the deceased's life are celebrated by guest speakers, and by collections of photos, and perhaps by a recorded message from the dead person.

The churches are full of flowers, the grave itself gets the same treatment. The clergy issue their platitudes, sometimes hymns are sung, and always there is a recorded series of favourite songs that were important in the person's life. There are often two services, one at the church and the other at the grave side. Generally, a wake, fully catered for, is available.

Comment. I could go on, but you get the idea. I do not deny that the dead and their families and friends have a need to grieve. And I do not deny their right to arrange any funeral they can afford and think fit.

But somewhere in me is an old fashioned cry for a return towards simple, more direct funerals.

Second comment. I note with a little bit of horror, how expensive funerals have become. **It's hard to know whether it is better to die or to get married. But this is a matter for debate some other time.** Perhaps later, in another period of self-indulgence, I might do this.

FEBRUARY NEWS ITEMS

Two twin girls, aged 22 months, drowned in a neighbour's swimming pool. The incident has provoked talk about the need for fencing of pools, and the introduction of tighter regulations on pool owners....

NSW had eight deaths from drowning over the last weekend.

The trouble in Ireland continued. Yesterday, British paratroopers shot dead 13 men and boys in Ulster as they marched unlawfully to protest against a Government decree that allows internment without trial....

In return, the four-story British Embassy in Dublin was set on fire and gutted....

Incidents as bad as this happen month after month, and usually feature members of the **Irish Republican Army (IRA)**. This a tough time for the Irish.

140 boys from a select boys' school at Coorparoo, near Brisbane, **were sent home for having long hair**. They were told not to return until their hair met a "short-back-and-sides" standard.

A Sydney woman has given birth to a baby girl in Sydney's Crown Street Hospital. There is nothing special about this, except that **she did not know until four days ago** that she was pregnant. Nor did her husband....

"I had no idea that I was pregnant. I just thought that I was putting on a bit of weight, and was thinking of going on a diet."

A Eurora grazier has earned the title of "World's Fastest Shearer". He sheared 410 merinos, in eight hours. The previous record was 347 merinos.

News from Londonderry, Ireland. An enquiry will be held into the shooting of 113 males here earlier this month. Military witnesses will be compelled to **wear wigs, dark glasses and false moustaches** so that they will not be recognised.

Tragedy in the scrub. A mother, father and 18-month-old child were stranded when their car broke down 30 miles from Eucla on the Nullabor Plain. They decided to walk to Eucla, and in intense heat, sheltered for a few hours in an abandoned car....

Later, with her husband exhausted from carrying the child, the mother set off toward Eucla, and left the other two in the car. Later, he recovered and staggered into town with the child. **But somehow she got lost, and died in the desert.**

An industrial chemist working with a large detergent company said that **the water in Sydney Harbour, around Balmain, contained two percent active detergent and five per cent phosphates**....

He claims that it could be concentrated three times, and a little bit of colour added, and **sold as active detergent** in stores and shops around the nation.

NIXON VISITING CHINA? QUITE LIKELY

There has been a lot of paper-talk this last month about the prospects of President Nixon visiting China. Reports are that Nixon will talk to the leaders of the Chinese Communist Party. And as well as that, the discussions will include top-level Russians. And then, supposedly, the Vietnam War will be all over, and peaceful hands will stretch across the oceans.

There are indications that the visit **will** happen. Diplomatic arrangements are being made, and all the necessary protocols observed. But **the bombing and slaughter of citizens and military** from many nations is continuing without any remission.

The big question being asked is how can any leader sit down and talk peace with heavy-weights who are, at the very time, killing their citizens?

The big answer is that it is simple. All the leaders are using the same tack. They say that there are problems facing the US and China relationship. One is Tibet. Another is Taiwan. Another is trade matters. And yet another is Vietnam. China now claims it is not directly involved in fighting in Vietnam, so that is just another matter for resolution with the US. But it will not be discussed in this visit. The agenda is now fixed to exclude **that issue** this time.

The sheer hypocrisy of this excuse is mind-blowing. China was still providing all the materials of war to the Vietnamese, it was providing all sorts of "advisers", and in some instances, active military assistance. Surely such involvement is worthy of discussion.

But the reality, the political reality, was that the Americans were stuck in a war that was getting more unpopular every day at home. Almost every American wanted to get out of it.

And for Nixon, this was an election year. He simply must pull some rabbit out of the hat. He needed good relations with China, and eventually peace in Vietnam, to do this.

So the two nations, acting just like civilised countries act, agreed to talks, at the top level, in mid-February.

AN AWNING GAP

The main streets of country towns are presenting a problem for local Councils. Any town of a decent size has a cluster of shops along the main street. Sitting cheek by jowl, they provide an amenity for shoppers to cruise along streets that are paved and guttered and level.

At the moment, some of the shops along the main roads have awnings. These provide shelter from rain, and hot sunshine. But some shops do not have these. So, people shopping need to struggle with their umbrellas as they go from shop to shop.

Many councils across the nation are now wanting to mandate that all such shops have awnings. Some of them go further and say that shops must all conform with certain standards that they define. For example, a town in the goldfields might have an old-fashioned look consistent with the 1850's.

In any case, some shop-owners want the awnings, and some do not.

Letters, J Allpass. I wish all architects who have designed, and are designing, modern city buildings would be condemned to plod along the City streets in the streaming rain without a fraction of cover from awnings.

The "brimless" public building is surely the worst architectural feature that has appeared in the past 20 years.

Letters, A Lansdowne. Joan Allpass wants architects who design buildings without awnings to be condemned to plod along the city streets in teeming rain. Might I suggest that, with its narrow streets, Sydney would look less tightly packed if awnings were eliminated altogether. One of the first things a newcomer to London notices is that few buildings have awnings, and despite the inconvenience when it rains, I believe that city and many others on that side of the world look better without them.

At the risk of hostility from those who would condemn the move, might I suggest that the city fathers consider whether removal of all awnings would result in an improvement in this city's appearance.

Comment. This is not such a problem in the big cities, especially where Government Departments dominate.

On the pavements there, the buildings run for hundreds of yards with no awnings in sight.

But in country towns, it is a matter for concern. Every medium country centre is now seeking to establish an identity, and good shopping conditions are important for that. There is no doubt that the pro-awners will win out in the long run. But the opponents, watching their dollars carefully, will keep the fight going for years.

Comment. I can go back to the early 1940's and remember the battles caused by suggestions that hitching rails be removed from outside shops. And about the same time, horse troughs were abandoned or moved out of sight.

Question. Do you remember hitching rails, and horse troughs? Where did all the troughs go?

GRANDIOSE GAMES

A Mr Moldan wrote to warn that Olympic Games were in danger of losing their role of championing sport, and at the same time, were putting unbearable financial burdens on those countries that sponsored them.

Letters, F Moldan, President, Sydney and Environs Development Association. From reports on the preparations for the Munich Games it is fairly evident that we are dangerously close to the stage where a drastic change in planning and organisation is inevitable if the Olympics are to be staged in the future at a reasonable cost, and are not to be abandoned altogether.

It is suggested that some of the principles which should be followed in any move on Australia's part to keep the Games alive should be:

(1) The preservation of the original spirit and dignity of the Games rather than their presentation in a luxurious, spectacular atmosphere.

(2) The building of sports complexes, including a transportation system to serve them, for the city's needs - not just for the Games.

(3) A similar principle could be applied to housing, for which there is also a constant need in this growing metropolis. With long-term planning, a housing scheme suitable for an Olympic Village could be built then used by the community after the Games.

(4) The Australian organisation concerned with Olympic planning should take the initiative in submitting a proposal to the International Olympic Committee to limit the number of sports, competitors, officials, etc, in order to keep the Games on a level which could be handled efficiently and economically.

We would be pleased to hear other suggestions as to how the present dangerous trend towards increasingly grandiose Games could be changed. If this matter is not pursued urgently Sydney will either be unable to act as a host city due to lack of suitable facilities at tremendous costs, or could organise the

Games on a somehow mediocre level - if they are still being held in 1988.

Here Mr Moldan had his eye on our proposal to hold the 1988 Games. We did in fact host the 2000 Games. Many different analyses wonder if they paid for themselves, and it is now obvious that maybe they did and maybe they did not.

But since Mr Moldan wrote, and warned, the Games have become more expensive, and have more athletes competing in more sports, and there are more advisers, coaches and managers and hangers-on than ever before.

Comment. Probably Australia is bidding for the 2032 Games. It would be wise to consider the spirit of Mr Moldan's Letter before committing to too much.

But, I think, it is unlikely that we will.

HERMAN IS SAFE - FOR A WHILE

About six years ago, a 7-foot crocodile escaped from the inventory of a travelling showman while in Lismore. Since then, it has been a feature of the nearby Richmond River.

Now, an artificial lagoon has been added to the River complex, and the croc has recently been seen in that lake. The Council reluctantly decided that human lives were more sacred than the welfare of a croc, and it should have it sent to a sanctuary in Queensland to be shot.

A huge outcry was heard from local residents, and a newspaper poll said the 90 per cent of the population objected to this.

In response, Herman the croc has been given a reprieve until the Council can get more information before it passes final judgement on its fate.

Comment. I can find no information on what happened to that croc. **Perhaps a reader of this book can tell me.**

WHAT IS THE ROLE OF TRADE UNIONS?

A controversy has erupted over the fate of a Sydney Church in Pitt Street. This was due to be demolished and a new church was to replace it. The Curator of the Church explained that this was in effect an Eighteenth Century Church, and was taking up a large part of the Church's income just for maintenance.

The Curator "added that finally we have decided that people were more important than buildings. That is so regardless of how ancient the building may be."

The Builders Labourers' Federation, led by Jack Mundy, argued that it was an integral part of Sydney's heritage, and it should thus be sacred for all time. And thus the Federation would refuse to demolish it.

But behind that argument was a matter of greater principle. In the bigger picture, it was about the right of **Unions to act on matters outside their traditional role of looking after wages and conditions of their members.** Suddenly they were moving on **to social issues that had nothing to do with working conditions.**

Here they were stating that the Trade Union had the right to say whether a particular church should, or should not, be demolished, and whether it should be rebuilt. This was a long way from the Unions arguing before an arbitrator for a three shillings wage rise.

So, the hackles of all concerned were raised. And so the argument got hotter and hotter. It spread to all sectors of the community during the Seventies. Jack Mundy and his Unions blocked project after project, acting as the final arbiter on whether buildings would be built.

Inevitably, the issue became muddied. Mundy was a dedicated Communist and so too were many of the unions that supported him. So for every building that was proposed and blocked, there were many cries that it was part of the Red plot to destroy the nation's economy. This served in turn to confuse the merits or otherwise of Mundy's decisions.

Comment.   In particular, there was a fear, especially among the alarmists, that the Builders could be seen as controlling all facets of the economy. That our established ways of government could be subverted by them, and our wellbeing could be determined by Communists.

PRETTY PICS FOR OZ

Australia is to get **colour** TV from March 1st, 1975. The Federal Government announced that broadcasting to all capital cities, and some country venues, will commence on that date.

The ABC will be ready for that date, and commercial Channels will be licensed from that date if they choose and meet technical standards.

The cost of a coloured set will be about three times as much as for black and white sets. It will not be possible to convert from one to the other.

FM radio is still not proposed.

PRIMING THE CHINESE PUMP

President Nixon is letting it be known that he will soon be leaving for Hawaii. He is taking stacks of files with him, and will spend two days there studying all aspects of US relations with China, and also keeping up to date with positions in the Vietnam War.

It is widely reported that there is little expectation that his visit to China will produce much of substance, but it will be **very important for telling China and the world that the American attitude to China has changed.**

A Special Ambassador will be sent immediately to Australia and the major regions in and around the Pacific. He will explain to these nations that the American complete change of face will not present any dangers to those nations.

Comment. This will take a lot of explaining. Nixon for years has based his political fortune on the American hatred of the Chinese. Many commentators are saying that Nixon's switch is purely to gain political advantage.

They stress that there is little advantage in his changed attitude, and lots of risk in abandoning his long-held position. The word " hypocrite" is often used.

On the other hand, there are those who say that all war is useless, that this particular war in Vietnam is most useless.

They ask, and ask, why would the US cling desperately to its old enmity when it could just as well have peace.

As is often the case, in the past, the present and the future, America was deeply divided.

NIXON GOES WEST: FEBRUARY 18th

Richard Nixon, President of the United States of America, has left his home country on a goodwill mission, that includes the one-time sworn enemy, China. US officials say that he will visit a dozen nations in the Pacific and Asia, and that Australia will be one of those nations.

His departure from Washington was marked by all the pageantry that the world expects from America. Hundreds of Congressmen were at the airport, and the same number of officials associated with the Cabinet. Thousands of school children had been given the day off school, and they were at the White House when he left there.

The propaganda machine was working full time. It now appears that "the Peking meeting with Chinese officials will climax years of secret diplomacy and public overtures behind the scenes". But, Nixon was able to warn that the road ahead was difficult, and that is would be unrealistic to expect American-Chinese relationships to be resolved quickly or easily.

Comment. So Nixon took to the skies in a welter of goodwill from the nation. We will pick him up again in a few days when he gets to Peking.

I add that Nixon's talks about secret diplomacy were indeed secret. In fact, hundreds of US personnel, who had been meeting with their Red counterparts publicly for years, were quite surprised that such diplomacy had ever occurred. A few suggested that they were a figment of an aspirational imagination.

NIXON CARRIES ON: FEBRUARY 22nd

Nixon and Chairman Mao Tse Tung enjoyed an unexpected meeting at the Chinese leader's Peking home today. A spokesman said that the talks had been serious and frank, but refused to give any further details.

Later at a banquet given for Nixon, Mao said that he hoped that normal relations between the US and China could be established soon. President Chou added that "Thanks to joint efforts, the doors of friendly contact can be open at last".

The whole scene was very low key. Just a limited number of Chinese officials that the US President gave his hand to, a few comments exchanged in a foreign language and at the airport, the US *Stars and Stripes* was unfurled on Chinese soil for the first time since the Communists took power in 1949. Some schoolchildren sang a song to Mrs Nixon. **None of the usual razzamatazz.**

Comment. Subdued but sensible.

NIXON FINISHES UP: FEBRUARY 29th

So matters went on for another week. Charming, not-too-cordial, a few banquets, Press coverage in China hardly visible, no crowds along the streets, a few gifts at the end, and then claims from both sides that everything went well, with just a suggestion by both parties that they had got the better of the other.

The two countries issued a joint 1,500 word communique that said talks had gone well, that we will make efforts to stay in contact. There was a reference to their differences over Taiwan that would prevent full diplomatic relations until matters were settled.

Nixon jumped in here and made the claim that "We have been here a week. That was a week that changed the world." Clearly he was a clever Dick.

Newspaper editorials across the nation, and indeed across the world, were unanimous in saying that talking was a good thing. They variously pointed out that the war in Vietnam has not been on the agenda, and that Taiwan had been on the agenda, but they had ducked.

Generally, editors said that it was a good start to rapprochement but, in the ever-changing world of international politics, events in the near future would be of greater significance than encouraging words in the present.

MARCH NEWS ITEMS

A battle is being waged between farmers on the one hand, and **manufacturers of table margarine** on the other. Our farmers are doing everything they can to cripple the margarine market before it gets a real foothold and reduces the sale of butter....

By law, margarine must consist of at least 90 per cent animal fat. If it is artificially coloured it would look just like butter, and at its cheaper price, would certainly gain a big share of the market....

The most recent skirmish made its way to the High Court. Those exalted judges decided to uphold a new Tasmanian law that **prevented the colouring and selling of the product**. It is expected now that the other States would adopt the decision as soon as possible....

But this is only one chapter in a saga that will go on for another decade.

Players of **brass instruments** are blowing their way to an early death. This is according to a study released in the US by the *AMA Gazette*....

The study showed that the average age of death for players of brass in the US, in the last three years, was 64. Versus non-players with an average age of 69.

Mr C J Cahill, **an Independent member in the NSW Legislative Council, made a speech that lasted three hours and 27 minutes**. He spoke at a rapid pace, and was not seen to stop even for a glass of water....

He was finally stopped by the President of the Council who decided that he was becoming repetitious.

A New Guinea family was moving to the Australian mainland , and were **appalled at the quarantine laws prohibiting their taking of their dog**. They decided to smuggle it into this fair land....

The family sought the help of an old friend, called Scott. He arranged for the Chief Engineer to hide the dog in his cabin. To quieten the dog, he tied its legs and bound its mouth. But it escaped, and hid on deck It was found by a helpful sailor who threw it to Scott on the wharf below....

He tucked it under his arm and ran away. All persons involved pleaded guilty and were fined a total of 1,250 pounds. And the dog was due to be exterminated.

Many of the larger cities in the States are having trouble in **burying bodies in existing cemeteries**. For example, a Bill was passed allowing for some remains in Botany, in Sydney, to be removed to another site to make room for other persons....

In the debate over this Bill, it was suggested, by Sir Asher Joel, that the bodies be removed from many Sydney cemeteries and **placed into large tunnels that would be drilled into the Blue Mountains.** He said that it would be necessary to do that, or else implement **vertical stacking one body over another**, in the one grave.

LIFE BACK TO NORMAL

Meanwhile, back in the suburbs and the country, life went on as if nothing had happened. People here, along with all the Editors, simply decided that this was probably one of those events that **came and went** every so often. It was clear that most of them thought that this would be one that **went**. "We will wait and see."

So, in this quiet month, I will take us off the international stage, and look at some of the glees and groans of everyday life.

BACK TO SCHOOL

Back in WWII, and the Fifties, there were very few controls placed on the day-to-day running of schools. It was generally considered that teachers were responsible, sensible persons who were wise enough to administer both lessons and punishment without any help from parents. A few schools, here or there, did form Parents and Citizens groups that were officially recognised by the school hierarchy. And a few parents did organise supplementary committees to run auxiliary functions, such as the school tuckshop. But, in general, the P and C was at best seen by headmasters as a decent sounding board, and at worst, a damned nuisance.

By the early Seventies, parents were much more concerned with the education of their children for a number of reasons. And this meant that there were many more parents who wanted their opinions heard by the school authorities, and lots of these parents by now were well educated and quite vocal.

But there was huge diversity from school to school and opinions differed about what their role should be. So arguments about all aspects of the P and C abounded.

Below is a sample of a few views on just one issue.

Letters, (Mrs) B Backhouse, President, Federation of Parents and Citizens Associations of NSW. It was indeed pleasing to read in the "Herald" the comment of the past president of the NSW Teachers' Federation that the morale of teachers was "pretty high"; to parents this is an extremely gratifying statement.

However, I must strongly disagree with Mr Whalan when he states that there is no place for a parent in the federation's concept of an education commission.

Parents are initially interested in education; and they are deeply interested in what goes on at their children's school. Parents may not be highly trained educators, but they are practical, level-headed people who want to know what the consumer is getting - and the consumers are their children.

Therefore, if the commission is to be responsible for general education policy there must be parent representation to watch the interests of the consumer.

Letters, D Reeve, Principal. As one who has been principal of a number of schools I have been unable to detect the deep interest in education that Mrs Backhouse claims exists among parents.

As principal of a school of 820 children I wrote, last week, to parents inviting them to a meeting of the P and C, at which I proposed to give a talk about why children perform differently at school and how they, the parents, could get the best out of their child's education. Twenty-eight people turned up; twice the average number. Six of these did not have children at the school, and others were husband and wife. A bare dozen families were represented.

Far more money is spent on cigarettes, beer, clubs, the "pokies" and gambling than on education, and these things represent the true interests of our society. I invite anyone to compare the amount of space devoted in Sunday's newspapers to horse-racing and spectator sports, and to education.

Such spasmodic interest that the average parent has in education is subjective, temporary and concerned only with her own child. In education, per se, interest is nil; Mrs Backhouse should stop kidding herself.

Since many teachers are also parents, the interests of parents on any education commission is assured.

Letters, D Peel. I have watched the growth of the influence of P and C's with great interest. I sympathise, in the first case, with the headmasters who know a great deal about almost everything that happens in the school. He knows the policies, and the implementation of them, he knows the idiosyncrasies of his teachers, and he knows just what children need careful watching. And he knows much more about the school than anyone else.

How galling it might be for him to be judged by a group of parents. Many of them are illiterate and ignorant of facts, many of them are just against the government, many of them are infatuated with their own children, and can not tolerate anything that displeases or disciplines them. As an ex-teacher, I can tell you that all teachers feel just the same.

On the other hand, some parents are measured and well-informed. From their perspective, they can see different points of view, and how galling it must be for them to be frustrated by an incompetent headmaster.

I expect that with further efforts on all sides, some system will be accepted by most parties. Then, as with all clashes between conflicting parties, balance will be achieved, but only for the periods where the parties are seeking honesty and behaving like sensible adults.

Letters, Joan Mulrony. I have just returned from America after teaching there for ten years in three High Schools.

Parent groups here are about ten years behind those in the US and in my last school occupied 30 per cent of the principle's time. They are populated by the very type of mothers that Mr Peel described, and on top of that, have generally devolved into factions that war continuously with each other. And look at the result.

Without moaning for pages, let me opine that the education given there is of a very low standard, and has no chance of improving.

Australia is ten years behind in school politics, and I hope we never catch up.

GAZE INTO MY EYES

In an article for the *SMH,* a journalist gave his opinions about the many aspects of hypnosis. He talked about stage hypnosis, in which several people from an audience appeared to perform remarkable feats under the influence of hypnosis.

He referred to articles from noted leading American students of hypnotic analysis, and progressively decided that they could be explained by factors such as careful choice of participants, and their will being reinforced by the hypnotist's power of suggestion.

He then talked about other uses for hypnotism, for example, medical hypnotism, and found that there was some evidence of their having significant outcomes.

He concluded that:

Article, D Gunston. As for medical hypnosis, the relationship here between the psycho-hypnotist and his patient is very complex and most doctors now agree that it is most difficult to pinpoint what achieved results may be due to hypnosis as such and to the other forms of therapy (confession, free association, etc) that are usually also involved.

Hypnotism, then, is now viewed by the scientific world as neither mysterious nor very special, while its usefulness for anything other than cheap entertainment is very doubtful.

The truth is that we just do not need the help of any mythical or superstitious forces in order to reveal our unusual or unsuspected abilities. If we can simply be persuaded we are able to do a thing, we usually can do it.

These were fighting words to the many believers.

Letters, A Burns, Applied Psychology, University of NSW. David Gunston's article "Is hypnosis any use?" should not go unchallenged, presenting as it does a most biased and inaccurate picture of the present state of scientific knowledge regarding hypnosis.

A detailed critique would be out of place, but the following inaccuracies are worth pointing out:

(1) It is true, as Mr Gunston points out, that the search for physiological changes occurring

during hypnosis has often been disappointing. This does not mean, however, that no such changes occur. It is just as likely that the measurement procedure has been inadequate to reflect the subtlety and complexity of the changes. In fact, recent research in both the US and the USSR has reported significant EEG alterations, during hypnosis.

(2) Persuasion does not appear to have at all the same effect as hypnotic suggestion. Any experienced hypnotist knows that the inclusion of even a small amount of persuasive argument in his hypnotic patter is likely to be fatal to success. Hypnosis appears to involve a suspension of the critical faculties of the subject - literally, a suspension of disbelief - and once the hypnotist abandons simple assertion in favour of persuasion the critical faculties and the disbelief are reinvoked and the hypnosis vanishes.

(3) The relationship between medical hypnotist and patient is certainly very complex, and good doctor-patient rapport is an essential; but the rapport and the hypnosis are not the same thing.

For instance, hypnotic anaesthesia has been used very successfully, in the dressing of third-degree burns, a very painful procedure in which chemical anaesthesia is sometimes out of the question because of the weakened state of the patient. Is it really sensible to ascribe such an effect to the doctor-patient relationship? If so, one wonders why the medical profession has bothered itself with the development of anaesthetics at all.

BABIES VOTING

Pressure was building up to allow people aged 18 to cast votes in Federal and State elections. The basic argument in favour of allowing this sprang from the fact that youths could be drafted into the military at age 18. Further, they could be sent overseas and forced to fight for their lives over a cause that they had no sympathy for.

Not only that, as had been shown in Vietnam, they could be killed. The punchline was that if you are old enough to be killed, you are old enough to vote.

This, at a time when young lads were being conscripted and forced to fight, was an enduring issue.

I enclose just three Letters showing some of the differences between people. The first is at an academic level, the second is more down to earth, and probably represented the preference of most of the population. The third I will make a comment on when appropriate.

Letters, J Evatt. The obvious procrastination of the Liberal Government in the matter of 18-year-old voting should be deplored by all who seek to maximise participation in our political system.

Survey data indicates that the result of such electoral reform would not necessarily be the substantial boost in ALP strength feared by some conservatives. In fact, the political complexion of Australian youth reflects with remarkable accuracy that of the wider society. However, the influx of new voters into the governmental system may pose a threat to some of the prevailing values. It would add a degree of the unpredictable to Australian politics and create a volatile, potent pressure group on issues relevant to youth, such as housing, credit and education.

The vote for young people may, to some extent, mitigate some of the alienation they feel from the conventional political parties. But, clearly, just as women had an arduous struggle to get the franchise, young people will need a vigorous campaign to achieve voting rights.

Labor has shown in its platform and statements that it is prepared to face the challenge. The onus, therefore, lies upon the State and Federal Governments to implement this change, which they have verbally supported.

Letters, June Gibson. Joan Evatt's Letter is perhaps worthy of consideration, but only at the edges. The principle question is should young men be allowed to vote. It has nothing to do with which youth votes for which Party.

If there had been no Vietnam war, it is probable that the question would not have been raised. If there had been war, society would not have chosen to give this privilege to the youth in question.

But there was a war. It highlighted the folly of existing practice. Not only the combatants but all those who missed out in the ballot, suffered months of anguish waiting for the lottery.

Every one of these deserve whatever benefits we can offer them, and that includes voting rights.

Females should not be left out. If circumstances had been different, they too would have been prepared to serve in whatever categories that were proposed.

They are all heroes or potential heroes, and they should be given the right to pick their leaders.

Letters, Tom Britton. People at the age of 21 do not have enough knowledge and life-experience to vote. Their minds are full of other youthful thoughts, and they do not have the experience to soberly think out the alternatives.

I suggest the voting age **be raised to 30 years**. And be limited to those with enough intelligence, and enough interest in public affairs, to imply that they are responsible citizens.

THUMPING YOUR WIFE IS FOR GOATS

I enclose the following Letter for obvious reasons.

Letters, D Verity. It is perhaps not without relevance to our impending plight in Australia when a friend writes to me from north-west Africa as follows:

Demetrication - abandonment of metrics - is going joyfully in Wotsitabia. After years of bondage to the metre, and the kilo, and all their accursed complications, the citizens of Omubowari (Omubo's Town - I was with him at Oxford), principal city of Wotsitabia, are delirious with pleasure at the restoration of their natural weights and measures.

Those restored include, notably, the thump, the wife-walk and the goat.

The thump is, variously, a measure of volume and weight, very complicated though not so complicated as the kilogram, based on the heft of the closed fist of an average Wotsitabian. A thump of well-made corn dough is a little larger than such a fist; a thump of lead, of a quality suitable for bullets, a good deal smaller.

A thump of feathers is about a foot cube when compressed by a maiden of average strength and swung to deliver a blow to the stomach equal in effect to that of the closed fist of a moderately angry man reacting to the customary Wotsitabian insult to his mother.

The wife-walk is a measure of length. It is the distance that a fairly loaded young wife will walk under the noonday sun in summer in the time it takes her husband to drink two sherbets in a reasonably cool tent, while discussing with a companion a moderately knotty point from the Koran on which the kadi has not preached for at least two moons.

The obvious complications of the square wife-walk as a measure of area are ingeniously avoided in the traditional Wotsitabian system by the use of a simpler measure - the goat.

The goat is that area of average desert (the Wotsitabian has no difficulty in recognising this) which will be fertislised year round by the dung off a reasonably well-fed adult goat not noticeably diseased.

The durability and intrinsic worth of the Wotsitabian system is proved by the fact that, after the introduction of metrics under the French devils, land still had to be sold in multiples of 1.73079 recurring hectares, which equals (as well as the French were ever able to understand these things) one goat.

APRIL NEWS ITEMS

A **survey conducted by the** *SMH* in Melbourne and Sydney showed that only 23 per cent of the sample supported the current system for National Service....

41 per cent want the current system, but without the requirement to serve overseas. **32 percent advocated scrapping National Service altogether**, and relying entirely on volunteers.

Charlie Chaplin is back in America. He left there in 1952 for a holiday in England....

The US Attorney General refused him a return visa until he **proved "his moral worth"**. The AG thought he was sympathetic to Communism....

He remained overseas until now, when he has been invited to receive an award at the Academy Awards ceremony. **His visa is now approved....**

His name will at last join the 1,000 American notable actors whose names were embedded in brass in the famous Walk of Fame in Hollywood Avenue. Not only that, but a statue of him will be unveiled....

Comment. It looks like he has survived the "**Better Dead than Red**" era that some powerful Americans promoted at the time.

The Victorian Government is introducing legislation that requires "youngish-looking" drinkers to sign in to bars, declaring that they have reached the age of 18. It hopes to thereby reduce under-age drinking.

Comments. Australians will **never** submit to any such proof of identity test. That would violate our civil liberties beyond reason. Never. No Way ....

Despite my comment, the Victorian Government is also considering extending the same proposition to the viewing of R-rated movies.

The normalisation of relations with Japan is gathering pace. We are conducting more and more trade with Japan, and long-term contracts are common....

We are now considering **removing visa requirements on Japanese citizens**. This will increase trade between the nations. But, importantly, it will open up the tourist trade into Australia....

But there are still many Australians who have not forgotten the War.

John Gorton was Prime Minister of Australia for the few years prior to William McMahon taking his place. He has now said that he does not expect to re-join the Cabinet after the next election near December....

This may be because he has never wanted the limelight and he just wants to serve from the back-bench....

But there is speculation that **he does not expect the Liberals to win the election**, and he does not want to be closely associated with them in their loss....

Watch this space.

THE LITTLE RED SCHOOL BOOK

An author in Denmark was able to cash in by writing a book that talked about naughty subjects for the education of schoolchildren. Its title is the *Little Red School Book*, and that title plays on the "Little Red Book" that Chinese General Mao Tse Tung was making compulsory reading for children in China. The Danish book has now made its way to Australian shores and in its modified form, is now on sale here. After a few days of selling, bookshops are reported to be sold out, and ordering extra copies.

Many people in authority are urging that the book be banned from all schools, and its sale not be allowed to minors. Some of the persons objecting have obviously never read the book, and are confusing its content with the glorification of Communism in Mao's volume.

Others are against the book because it discusses in detail many subjects that are taboo to most school children. But the book's publishers argue:

Article, David Dale. The book's stated aim is to help school students "make the best of a bad education system."

It suggests ways students can try to make school subjects more interesting and relevant to their needs, and it urges them to question critically what they are told and to have a say in how they are taught.

About 20 of the book's 200 pages are devoted to sex, and about 30 pages to drugs, including alcohol and cigarettes.

The remaining 150 pages contain masses of detail on such subjects as examinations, teachers' rights and duties, discipline, how the education system is run, intelligence, and different kinds of schools.

The book asks students to work within the system to achieve improvements by communicating with teachers and education authorities.

The book says students should use demonstrations and strikes at school only if they have tried every other method to get grievances settled. And it warns them to be prepared for punishment.

It also advises students never to "muck about" in class unless they are absolutely certain that the teacher is an incurable bore and they have tried every way to persuade him to change.

The section on sex uses the vulgar names for sexual organs, and describes sexual activities in the simplest way.

It includes such topics as masturbation, orgasm, menstruation, homosexuality, venereal disease, abortion and contraception (detailing different contraceptive methods).

The only "moral" advice on sex is of this kind:

"People who warn you against both strong feelings and sex are as a rule afraid of both. They haven't dared to do very much themselves, so they don't know enough about it. Or their own experiences of sex may have been bad. Judge for yourself, from your experiences."

Of pornography it says, "Porn is a harmless pleasure if it isn't taken seriously and believed to be real life. Anybody who mistakes it for reality will be greatly disappointed."

Under "Drugs," the book details many horrifying physical effects of tobacco, and concludes: "If you haven't started smoking, don't."

The book also sets out the dangers of alcohol, LSD, "pep" pills, morphine, opium, heroin and cocaine. It remains fairly neutral on marihuana, but says: "It can't actually solve any problems you may have; in fact it may just make them worse."

The final part of the book, on "School and Society," says that although changes are taking place in schools, they are generally made "so that people who have power can keep it."

"Teachers and students ought to work together for change," it says. "There doesn't have to be conflict between them. In fact, teachers have as little real power as pupils.

"In the long run teachers and pupils are on the same side in the struggle against the forces which control their lives.

"You can't separate school from society. You have to change one to be able to improve the other."

The Federal and State Governments all agreed that the book would not be banned from school libraries, though they all said that its reading would was not to be encouraged. Many authorities agreed that it touched on many topics that children normally did not discuss, but they thought there was no reason to refuse the information to the small group who would seek it out.

But there were quite a few who thought differently. These writers were adamant that the morals of the young could be tainted for life by indoctrination at youthful ages. Was this book a corrupter? Absolutely, said many. It was talking about matters that should never be discussed in public, it was preaching actions and thoughts that young minds should not be thinking about, it was challenging all the values and institutions that a stable society needed.

For those who thought this way, it was bad. Very bad.

Comment. Readers should remember that in 1972 many subjects were just not talked about. For example, the idea of anyone talking about sex was far too bad. And to go further and say that schoolchildren should be reading books about it, and then discussing them, was quite offensive to most of the population.

In the context of this book, the subject matter touched on topics that were simply not talked about, even by adults. No wonder the book caused such controversy.

As a Post Script, let me mention that the week after David Dale wrote the above report, the Victorian Police raided the last remaining seller of the book.. They took away the remaining 200 copies. At the moment, the distributors did not intend to send additional copies to Australia.

Personal Comment. I expect that on any issue there are people who take **conservative stances**. In 1972, when the world was getting more cynical about a lot of things, it was easy to paint these people as out of touch, or as fuddy duddies, or the like.

But these steadying influences play an important role in our society. They keep all of our feet on the ground, they provide a base level that we can start to rise from. If that base level was forsaken, and lifted much higher, progressives could well press on to even greater levels on non-conformism.

And of that, I am very wary.

NIXON? WHO'S NIXON?

A few days after Nixon left China it appears **as if his efforts have had no bearing on the Vietnam War.** Hostilities on a huge scale have opened up, and indeed carried over for months.

For example, on April 4th, the Press reports that the US is poised to launch the biggest air raids on North Vietnam since 1968. One senior US pilot said "when the weather clears, we are going to sock it to 'em".

All through the month, the newspapers carried headlines of the War. "*Reds poised for king hit*" on April 9th. "*Paratroopers fly into embattled Saigon*", on April 15th. Day after day the papers told of bigger and better conflict.

At the end of a month, Nixon gave a speech in which he said the US will continue its withdrawal of its land troops. An additional 24,000 army troops will be withdrawn by July 1st. But, because of the increase of hostilities in April, air and sea forces will be increased, by an unspecified number.

CROQUET IN WHITE

Over the years, many people have laughed at the uniforms worn by **women bowlers**. The term "white leghorns" is often used for them.

But it is not only bowlers who are under scrutiny. Uniform conservatism is also apparent in the fine game of womens' **croquet.**

Letters (Mrs) C Dynes. I would like to play croquet. It is a most civilized game.

But to play it in this country, it seems, I must wear the white uniform thought up by some hardly inspired person in the twenties.

Golfers have escaped this. They are not expected to wear plus-fours and check cloth caps.

Much of the charm of croquet, as played in other countries, consists of the visual delight of coloured dresses and balls on the green lawns.

If we must dress up, surely it would be more appropriate (and much more fun) to wear

Victorian bustles, striped blazers and straw boaters?

Letters, (Mrs) I Ferguson. I very much doubt the sincerity of Mrs C Dynes' expressed wish to play croquet, in view of her disparaging remarks regarding the dress customarily worn by its players here.

White for croquet has evolved over the years as a matter of convenience and expedience, as in the case of costumes worn by the players of most sports.

Dr Bray, eminent English croquet coach, who recently visited Australia, applauded the uniformity of our white wear, and hopes that it will soon become customary in England, too.

Would Mrs Dynes suggest tennis players forsake their white in favour of costumes of the days of Henry V, or that swimmers revert back to neck-to-knee costume, or cricketers to top hats?

The contrast of white on green lawns surely cannot fail to please her aesthetic taste. We of the fraternity of the mallet are proud to wear it, and have no wish to turn our sport into a fancy-dress party.

THE OPERA HOUSE STILL HAS FAULTS

The Sydney Opera House has been a source of controversy from the moment of its inception. Initially there were some persons who said that we were not big enough to have such a big House. Others said that the site, on an old tram shed, should be preserved for its historical value.

Then there was the selection of an architect. A swag of people thought that it must be an Australian, and that all aspects of it should be Australian-made.

Technical problem after problem delayed its construction. Scandal after scandal plagued its financing. The Opera House Special Lottery, run by the State Government, had many opponents. After all, the Lottery initially was to provide financing for hospitals.

Then it was taking longer, and longer, to construct. And the cost rose and rose. Utzon was sacked, with a lot of acrimony and protestations all round.

Now, **with its near-opening**, there was metaphorical singing and dancing in the streets, and the early reviews gave it a very positive thumbs up.

Was that the end of the Opera House controversies? Not by any means. Nitpickers abounded. Some of them even went back to the notion that it would be a flop, and that culture in Australia would not continue to support it. Every facet of it still had its critics.

Take, for example, these three Letter writers who focused their attention and wisdom on transport.

Letters, (Mrs) C Stewart. The official plans for a five-storey carpark to serve the Opera House have been announced and yet another opportunity to advance the public transport system has been sadly missed.

It would be of advantage to the community if the main transport to Bennelong Point were the existing railway and bus systems. This could be achieved by offering a reduction in fares to concert goers who either produce their tickets or request "an Opera House return." I feel certain that many would take the opportunity to travel free from traffic, parking worries and expense, especially if it is also of economic advantage to them.

The proposed moving footpath from Circular Quay Railway Station to the Opera House would give the necessary rapid, covered access needed to complete the movement of people.

The benefit is obvious - the Government Railways would gain patronage in off-peak hours.

Letters, M Cusack. Mrs Stewart speaks a lot of sense. The Opera House is the most awkwardly situated complex of entertainment in the world.

What happens to the last 500 cars if 1,500 car drivers deposit their passengers and then try to park in a parking station that holds only 1,000 cars? How long will it take to wait in the queue to enter the parking station? And how long will it take to walk from the car, finally parked, to the foyer?

The only way to make it possible for 6,000 people to arrive at the Opera House within half an hour is to have specially designed buses, free, as Mrs Stewart suggests, to travel from our railway stations, City parking stations and big hotels in a quick shuttle service.

Letters, L Rees. Controversy has arisen over the question of the expense and destructiveness - particularly in regard to tree growth - of the proposed carpark for the Sydney Opera House.

May I support the contention that such a carpark is unnecessary, in view of the amount of relatively free street space - especially at night time - between the railway and the Opera House.

Surely all this space could be declared a parking area at night for Opera House patrons?

And we might well remember the greater opera houses than the revised Sydney building will ever be, have managed to function very well without expensive concessions to the motor car.

The Sydney Opera House has been paid for by the general public of NSW and their interests in the shape of good public transport, should be a first consideration.

And in this regard - what about ferry transport to the building? (This was something Mr Utzon had well in mind.)

Few cities in the world can present such a thoroughly attractive proposition for theatre goers, and ferry services from all sections of the Harbour could well provide packed houses. Indeed, the Sydney slogan might well be - "To the Opera House by Ferry."

Comment. No one will ever know whether the site of Bennelong Point was the best site ever. But it has to be pretty close. The traffic problem is nowhere near to the picture portrayed above. And the grumbles and suggestions about transport are inevitable in a city the size of Sydney. The Opera House scarcely adds to that.

BEHAVIOUR OF POLITICIANS

Letters, M Kirkpatrick. Your editorial "The use of abuse" criticising the conduct of many of our members in the House of Representatives could to advantage be read and re-read by all our politicians.

I am prompted to make a constructive suggestion, aimed at improving the standard of debate and the general behaviour of our members.

It is that the Government parties should resolve that, during all speeches by members of the Opposition, no Government member should make any objection whatsoever; that interjections by members of the Opposition made during a Government member's speech should be ignored, except for a pause to enable the Speaker to call for order; that the **argumentum ad hominem** should be avoided at all times.

How conducive to grace and dignity it would be for a member to counter, during his speech, abusive interjections and cries by merely a pause and a raising of eyebrow. And how impressive would be an absolute silence on the Government side in response to abusive calls and interjections.

DEAD DUCKS

Margaret Meisenhelter was the Secretary of the Wildlife Preservation Society of Australia. She made the following points.

The licence period for shooting ducks in NSW lasts from February 19 to April 29, a period of 91 days. In NSW there are 60,000 licensed shooters. Each of them is allowed to shoot 20 ducks on the first day of the season, and 10 ducks per day on subsequent days.

Thus, making a few reasonable assumptions, it can be calculated that the number of ducks that were shot in NSW in last season was about **43 million**.

Adding to that, there were about 100,000 unlicensed shooters, and it could be expected that they would take more than licensed shooters.

She went on to say, as you might expect, that a study was necessary and that the governments should give the Society more money. **But the interesting news is the number of ducks shot.**

MAY NEWS ITEMS

The supersonic airliner, the Concorde, is being developed by Anglo French interests. It is due to start operation by 1974, but it is unlikely to fly regularly to Australia....

Flights from London to Europe and even Russia will occur, even though they lose money. The publicity they get will make them viable....

But not so for the more remote Australia.

The Australian Academy of Science had decided that **DDT can still be used in Australia**. The Committee who made this decision said that reviews of the situation should be conducted using data extracted from studies overseas....

In fact, DDT a decade later was prohibited in most parts of Australia because of its by-then established links to cancer in mankind and other creatures.

The **rock-musical *Jesus Christ Superstar*** opened in Sydney's Capitol Theatre last night. A small crowd of demonstrators from Church groups protested that "the **show presented Jesus as a human**, and in fact, less than a human."

Most of the audience saw nothing wrong with the show, and it became quite famous.

Question. Did any reader see this show?

Four hijackers were killed at an Israeli airport after they seized a plane with 100 passengers aboard. They were ready to explode the plane, within seconds, when

Israeli troops burst into the plane and shot three of them dead.....

This item is a reminder to readers that **plane hijacking was one of the most popular sports of the day**. It really made Australians nervous about flying.

The latest Gallup poll showed **that the Liberal Government had enjoyed a lift of two per cent**, and that Labor had suffered a similar fall. Elections are fast approaching, and people are starting to watch these polls anxiously....

This was the first such poll that the Liberals had won since March last year. **Are the Libs making a comeback?**

A well-known US State Governor, **Democrat George Wallis, was shot at an election rally**. He was seeking to win pre-selection as a candidate for the Presidency. He was hit by bullets three times, and apparently lost the use of his legs....

This is a reminder that **the US too is facing a federal election** later this year.

In Blacktown, in NSW, **three garbage collectors finished their all-night shift, running all night**. They saw a loaded soft-drink truck nearby. One of them took two 22 cent bottles of drink.

In Court, they were fined **a total of 300 Dollars**.

They were also sacked.

35-HOUR WORKING WEEK

Since before WWII, the working week was being reduced, from 48 hours per week in many of the labouring classes, down to the current level of 40 hours. Now Bob Hawke has popped up, and is talking about cutting hours to 35.

Let me make two things clear. **First,** Hawke's purpose was quite clear. There would be no reduction in wages. There would be no payback in requirements to work harder, or take fewer sickies. Just a reduction in working hours.

Second. If it was approved by one of the wage-fixing authorities in one industry, then it would be certain to be used as a standard for all employees everywhere, and within a few years, the entire wage force would have it.

You know without me telling you that employers were dead against it. And all Governments, being major employers, were against it. **And workers were all for it.**

The cat was let loose among the pigeons by an agreement reached between the Wharfies and their stevedore employers. This was most generous, and showed how desperate the bosses were to stop the rampant strikes.

In any case, **the agreement was made without any reference to any arbitration authority at all.**

Other employers and the Governments were outraged. The Federal Minister for Labour said that the agreement was "a cynical example of monopoly power. The Arbitration system has been bypassed, and the inflationary spiral has been given a new twist." He pointed out that all other employee groups will want the same concessions, and that the cost of overtime would rise by 12 per cent.

Hawke was not at all concerned about that. He said it would have little effect on inflation He went on to say that in five years **all industry would have a 35-hour week. This particular piece of news was not at all welcome to employers.**

Comment. Hawke throughout his political career was dedicated to the concept of direct bargaining. Even when he was Prime Minister, he thought that face-to-face negotiating was preferable to having outsiders make decisions.

In this particular case, he had many miles to travel before he could say that the 35-hour week was a settled part of the Australian scene. But he stuck it out and, as you know, most workers under awards now accept it as if life has always been like this.

NIXON IS TRICKY AGAIN

Richard Nixon is anxious to make headlines. Within this month, the American President adopted two positions that seem to be quite contradictory.

Firstly, he saw that North Vietnam was being serviced by 30 Russian ships that plied between the two countries, and was bringing in stacks of war materials to North Vietnam. So he threatened to blockade the ports involved, so as to stop the trade. And he threatened to blockade the ships still in the ports for the duration.

The President's anger with Hanoi showed in his use of such harsh phrases as "international outlaws," "arrogance," "insults," and "bombastic rhetoric."

Remember that Russia was supposedly not in the war, so this was an attack on a neutral country, so he violated dozens of laws and treaties, and was sure to enrage the Russians.

Secondly, while all this was continuing on the military front, a week later Nixon announced a definite plan about his intended visit to Russia. And on May 13th, he was received there, and some talks and a lot of banquets later, he left after a total of six days there.

But there were only superficial talks on Vietnam. We were told only that "the two leaders had lengthy discussions over Vietnam, the Middle East, and other issues."

So, back home in the US, public opinion was divided along the Party lines you would expect. It appeared that no votes were won or lost by Nixon's days out of the Office. Though the killing in Vietnam continued at the fastest rate this year.

MORE VIETNAM MARCHES

Australian University students had spent much of April watching President Nixon globe-trotting and meeting with the various people that he professed to despise. But now he was back in the USA, and was coming to the realities of an election in November.

Many Presidents over centuries have found that one policy that always got public support there was to **wrap himself in the flag**.

This means that he picked on a suitable enemy, and then vilified it. He did this by criticising its every move, real and alleged, starting trade wars with it, creating fear and distrust, and sometimes hints that a war was perhaps the only solution. And of course, there was only one way to avoid this. You can guess what that way was.

So, Nixon in this American tradition stepped-up his animosity to China. He applied the blockade of ports in any way connected with the Vietnam war, and this involved boarding vessels of countries like North Vietnam and China, as well as other nations supplying the North.

Students and Trade Unions **here**, deeply disappointed with the futility of Nixon's posturing, then turned out in numbers in May to stage demonstrations. These were the first such happenings for two years, and came as a shock to the general public who were hoping that this particular aspect of the war was behind it.

In any case, the demos went ahead in all capital cities. There were the normal punch-ups, and arrests, and accusations from girls of police brutality, and back to the pub to revel in having again saved the world. But the numbers of marchers totalled about 6,000, and they got good public support.

THE POLITICS OF SMOKING

The demos showed that while citizens were happy enough with the full withdrawal of our forces, and the partial withdrawal of US troops, they were still interested in seeing all conflict stopped, and were quite worried that the situation would reverse, and our men could be recalled to active duty.

Smoking tobacco was a national habit. By that I do not mean that everyone smoked, but about half the adult population did. And the other half more or less went along with them. People did not pull away with revulsion when a smoker lit up, people were rarely asked not to smoke in their houses, and people put out ashtrays for smokers' convenience.

Movies and magazines and newspapers all showed off the sophistication of smokers, and advertisements for the habit were everywhere.

In Australia, there were in 1972 a few people who were fighting to make smokers aware that their habit was in fact a health hazard. There was a growing resistance to smoking in the UK, but so far little of this had penetrated to Australia.

Professor Milton, a Professor of Surgery at Sydney University, made an effort through the *SMH* to **warn the populace**. He wrote a Letter that sets out the arguments that smokers use to justify smoking.

The arguments are:

That the health angle is not proven.

That there are many other health hazards

That the health industry is economically important.

The industry is making a legal product. Why should a legal product be restricted.

That in a democracy, why should not a person be allowed to smoke as he pleases?

Milton **then goes on to answer the arguments** and, as you would expect, he finds reasons in all cases to give up smoking.

He says that the tobacco companies, all of them world-wide organisations, are pushing these arguments on what is, basically, a gullible and ignorant public.

Comment. The Letter sets out clearly his answers to the points raised. And makes the valid point that smokers **only had to believe in one such argument to find an excuse for smoking**.

Of course, this was just the very beginning of the battle. Fifty years later, the population has now reversed its attitude, and the smoker is now often the pariah.

Comment. The NSW Government announced later this month that advertising on packets of cigarettes would be limited. That move will bring NSW into line with South Australia and Queensland.

Likewise, America in many States, and all of Britain, have introduced the same measures.

OLD POLITICIANS NEVER DIE?

Arthur Calwell came to prominence about 1940, and after 30 years in Federal Parliament, became Leader of the Labor Party in 1960. He held office until 1967, and sat on the back-bench until 1972.

He was notorious for the way he stuck to the pre-War values, and in particular, for his faith in the White Australia Policy for Australia. You will remember that in 1940 there were many Australians who said that Asians should **not** be allowed into Australia. This theory guided our immigration policy for the next two decades.

Early in the Sixties, however this nation started to swing away from absolute rejection, and was prepared to accept a quota of coloureds in each year.

This month, Calwell, no longer a Parliamentarian, described Asian migrants as having "10 or 12 children, they live on the smell of an oily rag, and breed like flies". You can see that he has lost none of his biases.

A number of people, many of whom rejoiced at the opportunity, raced to put the boot in.

Letters, L Siljegovic. So Mr Calwell is at it again.

I suggest to him that the sooner he retires and keeps quiet the better it will be for the Australian Labor Party and for all Australians.

So he thinks no red-blooded Australian wants a chocolate-coloured Australia? I am interested in the term "red-blooded" Australian. I didn't know any other kind existed.

As for a "chocolate" coloured Australia, it has never been anything else - a "wide brown land" originally inhabited by chocolate-coloured people. How does he intend to dispose of them? His remarks are an insult, not only to our coloured neighbours to the north - but to all those many Australians who do not choose their friends according to the exact shading of their skins but by their capacity for friendship.

So he wants to forestall any possibility of future racial conflict by keeping out all non-Europeans? I suggest we go a step further and exclude all adherents to the Catholic faith. In this way we can be sure to avoid troubles such as Northern Ireland is experiencing at present.

And let's keep out all socialists as well; then we will have no problems.

Letter, Ken Coutts. Would you not think that a man,who has spent all of his life hanging on to Labor's policies, would have enough sense to shut up right now. We have Labor fighting at the next election for its existence, and need every bit of public support it can get.

Yet we have Arthur Calwell coming out and using his spell-binding rhetoric and slanderous lies to attack good, honest, legal migrants.

If he had wanted to turn off Labor voters, he could not have done any better if he had tried.

Letters, E White. I, for one, and I believe the majority of Australians, support Mr Arthur Calwell's view on immigration, and he does well to remind the Labor Party and some Liberals that great Labor Prime Ministers like Curtin and Chifley and their predecessors stood four-square in favour of White Australia.

We have the glowing example of the turmoil and hatred caused by the colour problem in the United States and the problem in England, and particularly London, and many other parts of the world - and how with these examples before our eyes can we knowingly create the same conditions in Australia?

To our north there are aggregate populations of more than 1,000 million people, and what permissible percentage of this is it suggested to be let into Australia?

Five million would be a flea-bite to the 1,000-million-odd and of no use in easing the population pressure in their countries.

The same five million would, however, represent opening the floodgates on Australia's 13-million and ruin Australia's standard of living and accomplish nothing.

Why not let it be an issue at the November election, and doubtless the proponents of coloured immigration will get their answer?

Letters, P Collins. Our English teacher gave us a project, to write to the "Herald" about a topic we feel strongly about. I have chosen immigration.

Australia is one of the most underpopulated countries in the world for its size. It has only

13-million people and an area of 2,967,000 square miles, which is roughly four people to the square mile; but most of Australia being desert, it would probably be about 15 people. Australia has so many natural resources and not enough people to work them. I think immigration is a great thing because an immigrant from Europe will bring ideas with him, and people from the States will bring ideas from there.

But I do feel that there should be better laws regarding immigration.

Letters, M Greening. We assume that Calwell's next step will be to resign his papal knighthood. His views appear to us, as non-Catholics, to contrast sharply with those of the Pope.

MILK DELIVERY

Letters, E Jones. With my delivery of milk this morning, instead of 1/4 pint bottle of cream I received a printed pamphlet explaining that they had retired the "old girl."

Being an old girl myself, I object to the comparison with a 1/4 pint cream bottle.

What happens to people living alone who could not possibly use the 1/2 pint before it turned sour? Do I pour it down the sink to help boost an industry that is not prepared to help "loners" like me?

JUNE NEWS ITEMS

With Cracker Night approaching, Coles and other retailers banned the sale of fireworks in their stores. This is the first time that Coles has adopted this policy....

Woolworths will allow the sale of only small crackers and pretty, decorative fireworks. These bans are a response to the number of blindings and burnings that have marred bonfires in the last few years....

What a pity.

Passengers alighted from an aeroplane at Lydda Airport in Israel. While they waited to pass through Customs three Japanese gunmen shot dead 26 of them, and injured 72 others....

The gunmen were all Japanese, but they were mercenaries, with no allegiance to any country. They were acting on behalf of the Red Army, a Palestinian militia that fought as the bitter enemy of the Israeli State....

They had fired 180 bullets and thrown three grenades. Mrs Meir singled out Cairo and Beirut as places **where news of the mass murder was greeted with rejoicing....**

Maybe this was true, or just part of the propaganda and lies that both the Israelis and Palestinians poured out daily.

On the same day, President Nixon in Iran avoided a disaster when he was delayed by 45 minutes at a ceremony in Tehran. Two sticks of gelignite exploded at the site of the ceremony. One woman was killed, and several injured.

The French Government expects to drop its first atom bomb in the Pacific later this month. It will be one in a series at Mururoa Atoll....

Many inhabitants of the Pacific islands object to the tests, frightened by the possible health consequences....

A Professor of Biology at Sydney University says that it is inevitable that some Australians will die as a result. **"They will die from genetic defects, stillbirths, from leukemia, and other forms of cancer."**

The President of the ACTU has **placed a ban on Unionists servicing the French Concorde** when it arrives in Australia next month. It will be here as part of a round-the-world tour to promote the plane. Does that mean that the plane will not come to Australia?

The Little Red School Book will not go away....

Activist Sydney University students produced 2,000 copies of the book on roneoed paper and distributed it loose-leaf to nearby children on their way to school...

Police in Victoria raided book shops and seized all remaining copies....

In Queensland, the population was advised by the Government **that persons handing out rogue copies would be arrested,** and were liable to a jail sentence or a fine of $1,000....

What a wonderful gift of free advertising for the book. The battle over the 35-hour week continues. Hawke's victory did not hold up to scrutiny. While the various authorities noted that it had been agreed to by the parties, **it could not be accepted into law** until the wage-fixing Courts endorsed it. These courts of scrutiny said "no way"....

But dozens of Unions were now plaguing the Courts for the same benefits....

The militant Unions were calling 24-hour strikes to bolster their odds, and there is plenty of talk about major national strikes.

International pilots will strike next week for 24-hours unless the UN acts to stop hijacking of planes. Pilots in particular are worried.....

Their main grief is that some countries are offering sanctuary to the villains as ransom money. And that other countries are not following through on sentences handed out.

June 17th. The Concorde arrived at Darwin, two days ago. It was not too noisy, and the black smoke was not too bad either. But now it is **flying to Sydney**, on its way later today. Will it still be seen as acceptable? Will unionists refuse to work on it?

The nation is agog.

THE TEL AVIV MASSACRE

The politics of the Arab world was dominated by the enmity between Israel and the Palestinians. Ever since the Israeli State became a reality in 1948, and even long before, the two parties had vacillated between outright armed conflict and periods of very uneasy peace. Other nations, from Lebanon to Egypt, added to the chaos, and this region, often called the Middle East, remained a political and economic mess.

There were many citizens of the world who had given up on the region. They could remember the past 25 years, and before, when peace attempt after peace attempt had been reached by negotiation, and that was always followed by another big or small outbreak of actual war.

To be simplistic, to the outside observer, both parties wanted the same land, and it might be assumed that over time, some compromise, that would stick, could be reached.

But the whole situation was complicated by religious differences. The Jews on the one hand, and Muslims on the other. They had been fighting, under one regime or the other, for centuries, and the hatreds of those years were built into their politics.

It seemed to the same observers that nothing could ever change that state, and the best that could be done was to forget about it, and worry about getting the prawns for Sunday's barbie.

The people of the Middle East, however, could not be so cavalier. They were living surrounded by these realities, and their very lives and livelihoods depended on the outcomes.

So, to the people involved in the Arab-Israeli conflict, the incident at Tel Aviv was a just another confirmation that the war was still going on, and probably would continue for a long time. Would it ever end? Could there ever be peace between people who have hated each other for centuries? Could anyone outside broker a peace? When would the next outrage happen?

To people outside the region, everyone was shocked and apprehensive. I give you two views on this.

Letters, H Kahana. The lack of concern by the nations of the world at the massacre of innocent airways passengers at Lydda airport amazes me.

Are the nations, including Australia, so complacent that they believe that this could not happen at Heathrow, London, Idlewild, New York, or Mascot, Sydney?

There has since been a report of a hijacking for ransom in the United States. In Australia recently there was the Mr Brown incident. And yet the nations remain silent, awaiting some dangerous lunatics to commit outrages on their own soils, similar to the outrage at Lydda.

It behoves the world's Governments and the world's press to raise their voices in protest and to take measures for the security of all airways passengers throughout the world, and to take measures against nations who harbour and even encourage violent lunatic fringes who endanger transport and navigation.

Continued silence encourages lunatics, hijackers and pirates. The time to speak up and act is now. Tomorrow may be too late.

The murder of innocent Christian pilgrims and others at the Tel Aviv international airport by agents of the Arab terrorist organisations is an act which must be condemned by all civilised nations.

While Lebanon and Egypt have expressed their glee at this murder, Lebanon must bear the full responsibility, for it is there that these terrorists were trained. It is quite clear that as long as the Lebanese Government gives training facilities to murder gangs, in defiance of international law, such outrages against air travellers will continue.

Air travellers are entitled to insist on security from such attacks, and Governments must take concerted international action to annihilate the facilities and training camps used by these piratical murderers.

Letters, Abe Lawson. These writers are asking for governments of all sorts and all nations to combine to stop the terrorist activities. This is a good call.

But these writers, and so many others, focus on a recent incident, and by implication, imply that if you could fix the matter under question, then the whole problem would go away.

Of course they are not wrong to reply along those lines. But so often, the basic nature of the problem is lost in trivial detail, and the full problem is ignored.

I say this with the experience gained in the next 50 years from this Tel Aviv incident in 1972. The basic remains the same. The hatred generated over centuries still remains, and so too do the religious differences. And hence the war-like events still mar the lives of those nearby.

Comment. I have no solutions to such a massive problem All I can say is that I, like so many people in the Middle East and the world, live in hope that something, somewhere, or someone, will find a way towards lasting peace in the region.

STILL NO PEACE IN VIETNAM

Australia withdrew its troops from Vietnam towards the end of last year. But the issue has not gone away. See, for example, the riots in our capital cities last month.

And see too Letters like the one below that constantly turn up in the newspapers.

Letters, D Syme. The current mass bombing of both North and South Vietnam indicates that the Americans do not discriminate. One has only to travel abroad and mention one is from Australia, to be asked immediately why our troops were ever sent to Vietnam. They have been back only a few months and latest reports indicate that the province where they were stationed is already being overrun by the Provisional Government (Vietcong) forces.

The fact that the Australian Government has flatly refused to send troops back to Vietnam would indicate a change in its position, too.

Mr Harries should also consider a change in his attitude and join with the growing movement throughout the world urging that the Vietnamese people, whether in the North or South, should be allowed to determine their own future without interference.

Comment. There were many Australian families who lost interest in the war as soon as their sons and their mates came home. Many other pacifists took the same attitude. But there were other pacifists still as fiercely opposed to the war, and would fiercely oppose it till its very end.

For many of these, their opposition could have been based on opposition to all wars. And indeed, it was in some cases. But for the majority of those who were now against the war, not involving their own soldiers, it was based on the belief that this was America's war, that we should have had no part in it, and that they would never rest until all traces of that war were gone. Mr Syme, above, fits into that category.

Second comment. Everyone could see that there was absolutely no point to the war. But it is a sad fact that it continued on, slaughtering civilians and military alike.

TRADE WARS

The world was changing. I suppose that does not come as a shock, but one aspect where change was very apparent was in the world of corner stores and the new, brash, arena of **chain stores**. People who had previously bought their groceries and tobacco at corner stores were starting to buy them in snappy new premises that also traded in clothes, and records, and appliances. A whole host of new merchandise became available in a single shop, often some distance from home, and the friendly daily shop at the corner store changed to a twice-weekly visit to the chain store.

In 1972, there was still a long way to go in this transformation, but it was showing up to a degree everywhere. The local chemists felt this early on.

Letters, M Bradley. If it is good enough for chemists to sell nylons, pantyhose, sunglasses, bathing caps, cameras, films, furniture polish, shoe dye, confectionery, toys, etc, they can hardly expect the chain stores to pass up the opportunity to sell certain patent medicines, and probably more cheaply too. As long as the chain stores don't trade in drugs, I cannot see the chemists have anything to complain about when they encroach on other than medical lines.

Letters, P Jellard. M Bradley would not be in such a hurry to condemn chemists if she/ he considered the facts over the issue of chain stores selling certain chemists' lines.

There are two main points:

(a) I doubt if any chemist could afford to stay in business and offer (as he does in a majority of cases) a valuable public service if he relied on trading in drugs alone. This is why he has to sell other lines. However, does this apply in reverse to chain stores?

(b) Unlike his other professional colleagues - the doctor, solicitor, etc - no chemist, by law, is allowed to charge a professional fee except for the 70c which he receives for dispensing prescriptions.

My chemist in the City still finds time to dress wounds, remove splinters, offer anti-nausea medicine and give advice (but never encroaching on a doctor's territory), mostly to a lot of people who appreciate and value his services. Of course, he often finds those who are too mean to go to the doctor and walk out without so much as a thank you. Furthermore, many lines stocked by my chemist are cheaper than some items already carried in chain stores.

No, I dread the day when I end up with the vegetables on one side and the lingeries on the other, to try to obtain some professional advice as to the effectiveness of certain medications.

Comment. Of course this just was the beginning. Clusters of new shops became plazas, market-towns, and Northgates. The little man, the corner store, the one man shop and business, gave way to the giants, with a few brave sole traders and family partnerships struggling along beside them. Later, the disease spread and the giants became shopping centres, with franchises, and chains, and vast parking areas,

What a difference 50 years can make.

IT TAKES YOUR BREATH AWAY

Random testing of drivers was being mooted by a few persons. The argument for them was that so many people were being killed and maimed on the roads that society had to bear a burden to stop that. The counter argument was that our civil liberties would be eroded.

The influential *SMH* left no doubt about what it thought.

Editorial. It is depressing that two State Cabinet ministers, Mr Maddison and Mr Jago, have come out in favour of random breath tests to detect drinking drivers, but reassuring that the Minister for Transport, Mr Morris, maintains his firm, often-stated opposition to them. "I would be highly offended if I were going on a picnic with my family, stone cold sober, and was hauled out into a line for a breath test." He would be right to be offended, and so would anybody with any character.

It depends, of course, what they mean by "random" tests. Completely at random? Anywhere, at any time and without reasonable grounds? If so, there is absolutely no case for such a provision, which would smack of the police State. It would be as bad as stopping somebody in the street, utterly without reason, and searching his briefcase or her handbag for a banned book or a dangerous drug. The innocent must not be confused with the guilty. Law-abiding people must be free to go about their affairs without police badgering.

But perhaps they are thinking of something much more limited and circumscribed - such as in Britain, where the original proposal for completely random tests has been greatly watered down; or in Victoria, where there seem to be some restrictions on police action. But surely the test must be that police should be obliged to have a good reason for enforcing breath tests. Anything less should be totally unacceptable.

Comment. Wow. Talk about things changing over 50 years.

OPINION ON CONCORDE

The big bird has come and gone. It has, however, left behind a society much divided about its value and future. Of course, given the epoch-making nature of such an aviation advance, it could hardly be different.

I give you a sample of what readers thought.

Letters, D M Dennis, President, Royal Aero Club of NSW. Most technical advances through the ages bring new real problems in their train, and these are inevitably solved. However, at that time there is never a shortage of imagined problems which many people, in their understandable ignorance at the time, are ready to worry about.

Let's look at a few. Iron boats surely must sink because it's abnormal for iron to float. Henry Ford's contraptions will pose a great danger to all the cities of the world with tanks full of petrol roaming the streets. Columbus's ships will fall off the edge of the earth when they get far enough west. If man was meant to fly he'd have been born with wings. If we don't have neck-to-knee swimming costumes, there will be mass rape on every beach.

It all looks foolish now, with the advantage of hindsight, but there have always been plenty of genuine worriers, habitual knockers or plain hysterics to form a large bandwaggon and there probably always will be.

Some of today's Concorde worriers are attributing possible problems to the aircraft associated with altitudes that it will never reach. Some of them worried about the sand dunes that would be mined to provide the titanium metal for Concorde. Unlike the proposed American SST, Concorde is an aluminium aircraft which will use only about 7 per cent titanium.

The worry list is endless, most of it baseless.

The public, therefore, may gain comfort from the expectation that if and when the Concorde becomes a regular form of public transport operating to and from Australia, it will do so only after having proved to be capable of performing with all due regard to the public interest.

Letters, R Foot. D M Dennis wrote of the uninformed distortion of facts connected with the Concorde. I support his views, since I believe Concorde is only a minor pollution issue.

Author Robin Boyd said that until it is as slow and uncomfortable to move between London and Paris as it is to move between London and Sydney, Marshall Mcluhan's "global village" is nonsense, a fake, a northern hemispherical trick.

The speed of this aeroplane represents a major step in narrowing the psychological gap between Australia and the Western world. We will only find our level on an international basis if leading Europeans and Americans can be persuaded to come here instead of playing a sometimes patronising host to our emissaries.

We want an independent cultural identity, but not one out of touch with world thinking.

Letters, (Mrs) C Dynes. The reactions to the demonstration flight of the Concorde reminded me of the reactions of the animals in "The Wind in the Willows" to the early motor cars.

"What grace! What speed!" cried Mr Toad, who can hardly wait to climb into it. The sagacious Badger and Water Rat have grave reservations, whereas the Mole will go along with everything and everybody.

Unfortunately, the Mr Toads of this world, being so much richer than the rest of us, usually get their own way.

Letters, A Pritchard. In all the controversy over the Concorde, and particularly with regard to sonic boom, I am surprised that no one has mentioned the fact that this phenomenon is with us already, and is here to stay.

Our Air Force is surely equipped with supersonic aircraft, and does anyone imagine for one minute that our "flying fortune," the F111, as it races from coast to coast in defence of these shores, will be preceded by a man waving a red flag?

Letters, F Davidson. Please add my voice to protests against the Concorde. Having now experienced the vile and frightening sound of this aircraft travelling over my head I am no longer open to arguments in its favour.

Comment. One or two of these Letters had some points worthy of argument. But most of them had little of merit. Still, they do collectively say a lot. That is, after all the hype, of near-disaster, there was no sign of the public outcry now forecast. The masses of people that would have their lives changed by its presence did not cry out in anticipation of permanent misery. The budding environmentalists were no longer dismayed by fables of huge emissions blanketing the skies.

The big bird has gone away. So too has the frenzy of opposition that came with it.

JULY NEWS ITEMS

At Saigon airport, **a hijacker demanded** that the plane be diverted to Hanoi. After a scuffle, he was shot dead by a military passenger who was carrying a gun.... Many people are saying "Good. **Decisive action at last**".

Opposition to Bob Hawke's plan for a 35-hour week continues. The heads of the coal industry are warning that such a move would make mining more expensive, and force us out of overseas markets. That would hurt the nation.

A group of six teenage boys and girls heard persistent rumours that **a large country house was haunted**. They waited for the occupants to be away for a weekend, and occupied the house looking for ghosts. After several hours there, they were arrested, and fined $50 each for trespass.

The leaders of **North and South Vietnam are having talks** that suggest they can bring about a peace settlement. This is without any outside involvement from other nations such as America. This news is welcomed by all nations, and everyone is holding their breath.

Australia and Indonesia have few disputes. One of the few outstanding concerns is about where **the boundary between the two nations sits**, near Timor. It is known that the Timor Trough holds vast reserves of oil, and so the boundary between the two is important....

On-and-off talks are continuing between the two countries. And in fact, the matter will be scarcely settled fifty years later.

Three men are planning to walk the 1,100 mile Canning Stock Route through the Simpson Desert in Western Australia. They are trying to pull a cart, loaded with 12 lbs of water and 160 pounds of food, across the Simpson Desert....

The land has been abandoned by Aboriginal tribes, camels and kangaroos because of a lack of water. Most observers describe the trek as impossible....

Police have asked the men to abandon the attempt. They are motivated by fear for the lives of the three, and also by the high cost of search and recovery if things go wrong....

Not at all deterred, **the men will continue**.

There is **a mouse plague in the Darling Downs** in Queensland. An American, from Tennessee, has offered farmers once cent per live mouse. He aims to get a plane-load, and fly them home as pet food for crocodiles...

He has not yet worked out how to capture so many mice, but he is working on a solution and is encouraged so far.

OUR SUNDAYS NOT SO BRIGHT

Australian cities on Sundays had a world-wide reputation for being the dullest you could find. Part of this stemmed from the influence of Churches that wanted to keep the Sabbath sacred for contemplation, for prayer, and the family. Some of it was the feeling that it should be simply a day of rest, without the stresses that were generally being felt in a busier world.

In any case, they were dull. No pubs, no cafes or restaurants, few sporting fixtures, and no fees collected at the gate. Limited bus and train services, very few theatres, sometimes a good Christian theme for performances at the Town Hall. It all varied from State to State, but our cities were dull, very dull.

So, the Letter below offered some hope.

Letters, B Maguire. While on the subject of the New South Wales Art Gallery opening all day Sunday, why not mention a few other amenities which could provide a service to the public on the one major day of rest?

I do not want people to work their lives away, but surely some system could be devised to help the general public spend their leisure time.

For instance, why do most commercial art galleries close on Sundays? Not only do I find this peculiar, but many tourists from overseas agree with me. And what about book stores and record shops? And more cinemas opening their doors, particularly with continuous sessions?

Last Sunday I was in the City and it was most heartening to see the crowds of people wandering through the new Centrepoint complex - and, joy of joys, a coffee shop and a card shop were actually open; and from the people inside, it looked as if the owners were finding it worthwhile.

There seems to be an attitude in Australia that whenever a Sunday or a public holiday looms on the horizon, everybody closes down. Let's liven up our City and give people more enjoyment - much more choice than a handful of galleries, a few cinemas, the beach, reading a book, taking a walk and going visiting.

THE 35-HOUR WEEK

As we saw, Bob Hawke started talk about the 35-hour week a few weeks ago. He appeared to make gains in one case, but the Federal Government let it be known that the idea was not acceptable, and that the Government would oppose it.

That was not the end of the matter. Once that can of worms was opened, the concept became widely accepted among working classes, and strongly opposed by bosses and governments.

Arguments flew back and forth. There were the obvious ones. How much the extra wages bill would be increased? Would it break some businesses? What would happen to the cost of commodities? It would help the so-called workers, but what benefits would the rest of the nation get?

There were lots of ideas, some of them sensible.

Letters, N Izett. As manufacturers, wholesalers and retailers each have to add at least one-third to provide for premises, taxation, and wages, a quick calculation will show that, especially if sales tax is involved, the extra $1.43 can result in an extra $4 for the customer to pay.

Letters, G Lane. For heaven's sake, cannot Mr Whitlam see that Australian industry is just unable to afford such plans? Or is he simply overpowered by ACTU manipulations of his policy? Any citizen with foresight can see that the whole idea behind a 35-hour week is not more leisure time but a greater opportunity for overtime payments. I cannot believe for one minute that Australian workers will accept a lower wage for fewer hours worked.

If Labor manages to scrape into office pledging such "benefits" as a 35-hour week, it will face an even bigger task of controlling inflation than the Liberal Party has in its current term. A 35-hour week must mean higher costs for manufacturers and hence even higher prices for consumers.

Other writers saw the situation in a more complex light.

Letters, P Vermont. It is tragic, I think, and most unfortunate to this country that our managers cannot think of anything else as part of their managing jobs than to pass to the customer all cost increases immediately they occur, then sit back in their armchairs and relax.

I have serious doubts that the characteristics of this type of management thinking can be justified. Somewhere in the back of my mind I visualise a hard-working progressive manager (could this be fiction?) who not only is qualified and able to manage, but shapes the thinking; a trouble-shooter who overcomes problems.

He, in this case, would reorganise the flow of production, re-plan the operations involved and/or replace the old, long ago fully written-down, obsolete equipment with modern machines and produce nine or 10 cabinets in the 35-hours to keep the extra profit for his company. How about that?

Surely Mr Izett cannot prove that the present production method, with eight cabinets in 40 hours, is the most advanced, a non plus ultra with no further improvement possible.

If managing is so very simple - only a recalculation of prices to pass on the burden to the public - it makes me wonder why managers are needed. I am of the opinion that they have to do a lot better than that.

Letters, A Ward. In all this flap about the 35-hour week I have seen no one bring up the question: What happens to shiftworkers if a seven-hour day becomes accepted?

Do they work seven hours normal time then one hour overtime? If so, this makes them work a 40-hour week after all, but one presumes this is not important as they work a compulsory overtime day shift each month now; another 15 hours a month "only" increases costs to the customer.

Or do they work seven-hour days, with the shift times slipping back an hour each time, three hours per day? If so this will raise a howl of protest because regulating shiftworkers' lives is hard enough now.

Or do they work seven-hour days, and during the odd hour before the next shift arrives allow the staff of the company to keep equipment running? I shudder and draw a veil over the possible results of **this** alternative.

The possibilities are endless, but what is the answer?

None of these 35-hour agitators can beat the mathematics of 3 x 8 = 24. It's one thing they can't change.

Comment. So, the disputes went on. They were in general not very illuminating, but then a sudden decision by the mighty Commonwealth Arbitration Commission found that, for the 15,000 **waterside workers, a 35-hour working week was now the standard.**

Let me interrupt the flow of this story to clarify for you the responsible roles of the parties. **The Commission** was the recognised trend-setter amongst all the arbitrators, boards, tribunals, and Commissions that the various States had established for settling disputes. What ever it decided, the dozens of other agencies ultimately followed.

The waterside workers had one of the two most militant Unions protecting their interests. Again, a decision in their favour would certainly flow through to unionists everywhere.

Bob and his merry men were merry indeed.

Of course, the Commission was at pains to say that this decision would not automatically flow on to the other Unions and Awards and the States. Nope, this was a special case, no flow-on would ever be considered.

This was just a fiction. Everyone knew that it would flow on, and that the 35-hour week was just around the corner for all workers.

WHO CAME FIRST?

Everyone who went to school in this fair land during my childhood learned at least one essential fact.

That is, that Australia was discovered in 1870 by Captain James Cook. A few other sailors dithered round the edges and have proponents that claim it was not Cook at all. But, to my generation of school boy scholars, it was one James Cook that has the honour of being "The Discoverer of Australia."

Over the years, a few doubts have been raised over this claim. The Dutch have often been mentioned, and more recently, the Chinese have been added to the list of possibles.

Recently, an article in the *SMH* raised the issue again and added rumours of the Portugese and even the Arabs.

It settled on the Chinese as the very first to land here, and record the landing on maps.

But, as usual in this debate, someone else had a different theory. I will leave him to entertainingly speak on his own behalf.

Letters, R Gilroy, Director, Mt York Natural History Museum. I was most interested in the feature article, "Did the Chinese discover Australia?"

Ancient Chinese navigators were indeed here.

Chinese navigators were trading with the islands of South-East Asia centuries before the birth of Christ.

The Javanese, with whom the Chinese traded, had an extensive knowledge of our northern waters. They were probably instrumental in directing Chinese, Phoenicians and other ancient seafaring races to our shores.

Many ancient Chinese expeditions through Torres Strait came to grief due to the dreaded

Torres Strait Islanders who, until early this century, were head-hunting cannibals.

In fact, the islanders regarded Chinese as being just about No 1 for flavour, as they found them not as salty as white men.

Twenty years ago a jade Buddha was unearthed 75 miles from Cooktown. Five miles from this site is an ancient Aboriginal engraving upon a rock-shelter wall depicting Buddha, over which red ochre has been sprayed. It is evident that Chinese were thereabouts long enough to influence the rock art of the local Aborigines.

There is evidence to suggest that ancient Chinese once sailed up the Calliope River inland from Gladstone, Queensland, to mine for gold centuries before European settlement.

In 1970, evidence came to light near Sydney suggesting that ancient Chinese navigators had been in the Hornsby region. Aboriginal rock art of that area depicts human figures dressed in garments typical of early Chinese seamen.

In Taiwan Museum there is a map dating back 2,000 years showing the southern coastline of New Guinea, the east coast of Australia as far south as the Melbourne area, and the crude outline of Tasmania. There are other maps dating from the same period and earlier, including one showing the complete (though crude) outline of our entire continent.

Indeed, there is plenty of evidence to show that Australia was a land known to the ancients centuries before the first European voyages.

I believe our history books will soon **need to be revised** to show that Vikings landed on Cape York via the Solomons 700 years before Cook; that ancient Egyptians, in vessels navigated by Phoenicians, landed on the Kimberley coast 3,000 years ago, giving much of their Osirian religious philosophy and other elements of the their culture to the local Aborigines.

Our history is older than we often realise.

Comment. I have seen no sign of the forecast revisions.

LADIES AND GENTLEMEN: BE SEATED

In various States, authorities were fumbling with the concept of compulsory seat-belts. Should they ever be used? Perhaps only in front seats, or only in the driver's seat. Should children have special-sized seats just for them?

There were also questions of civil liberties. Were compulsory belts a violation of our concept of civil liberties? On the other hand, the refusal to wear them by a driver puts other people at risk. And a refusal by passengers places a burden on other members of a family and on people who have to rescue them. And also on the public purse.

There were other suggestions. Remember that at this early stage the belts were not retractable, and just lay about on the seat when not in use. Nor were they constrained at the shoulder. Just lap belts really.

Letters, Tess van Sommers. When is some car maker, or manufacturer of seat belts, going to provide us with belts in distinctive colours, so that one is not for ever fumbling for the right end of one's seat belt?

For a start, how about red and green (port and starboard) webbing? Or, where three sets of belts are provided front and back, how about distinctive colours on each set of buckles, or even fluorescent numbers?

Letters, H Turner, Traffic Engineering University of NSW. Tess van Sommers asks for differently coloured seat belts to avoid confusion.

This may be said to be a bad idea because it will prolong our acceptance of this crude and clumsy way of implementing a scientifically sound method for occupant restraint during a collision.

Let us press for properly designed individual seats, each with the belt built-in and retracting into the seat when not in use. This has been demonstrated to be practicable. When in use the belts will fit the wearer snugly and so be more effective when needed.

The present untidy mess of webbing straps will be eliminated.

Letters, F Lawson. Why are the buckles on seat belts not standardised?

This would prevent fumbling and consequent waste of time in emergencies, when they have to be unfastened by passengers unfamiliar with that particular clasp, or by strangers assisting at an accident.

Comment. Sadly, even fifty years later, a few still do not wear them. But not because of civil liberties.

WOMEN SHOULD KEEP TO THE RIGHT?

On escalators, should there be one rule for certain women, and a different rule for everyone else? That does not seem to make much sense if you are trying to make pedestrian traffic flow smoothly.

Judge for yourself.

Letters, T van Sommers. P Carne attacks the idea of directing people to stand on the right on escalators, as is done in London.

The London rule of standing to the right on escalators (distinct from keeping to the left on the roads and pavements) is sensible and practical because it takes into consideration the dilemma of women and their handbags.

For generations women have tended to carry a handbag looped over their left arm. They also tend to carry such things as gloves and small parcels in the left hand, leaving the right free for helping themselves on and off transport and for most of the gestures of shopping.

Many women want to steady themselves as they step on and off an escalator. If the rule is keep to the left, they have to transfer all their impedimenta to their right arm in order to do this steadying - and, moreover, use the left hand, which is normally not used for such aid.

Many Sydney escalators already have a "Keep to the Left" sign. It is generally ignored by women, for the good reasons outlined above. My advice to all women is to ignore pressures to make them stand to the left on escalators and to adopt as their motto in this situation, "Dieu et mon droit."

Letters, Tom Bain. What a silly idea in Tess van Summer's letter. Keep to the right on escalators if you have a handbag, she says. Let the plebs keep to the left. But who will control the traffic chaos that will ensue? How can anyone overtake?

Comment. Mr Bain is being silly. The simple solution is to have escalators for men and women with handbags, and other escalators for those who do not.

AUGUST NEWS ITEMS

A rich elderly spinster died in Florida in 1968. She left **four million dollars to 150 stray dogs** she was keeping. The family have been fighting the will on the grounds that she had lost touch with reality....

The Courts have now found that the will can stand. **The dogs are to be housed in canine luxury.** 69 of them have died, and the remainder will be tattooed to prove they are part of the original pack....

This arrangement will last for 20 years, and then the family fortune will go to a University in Alabama.

Seventeen men were killed underground when two explosions rocked the Box Flat Colliery, near Ipswich in Queensland....

A few of the dead were not killed by the explosion, but had to be abandoned because of the dangers and gases that still existed. The shaft will probably never be opened again....

This is **the worst mine disaster in Queensland since 1921** when 76 were killed at Mount Mulligan.

American citizens **living in Australia** will be able to vote in the upcoming US elections in November. There are about 65,000 persons who will gain this right for the first time....

Comment. That 65,000 is much higher than I realised.

The Labor Party's slogan for the coming Federal elections has been released. **The slogan is "It's Time".** Simple though it may be, it has become famous.

A Gallup poll indicates that **half the Labor voters supported the 35-hour week**, and only 30 percent of the Liberals did....

Those who supported it said that it would reduce unemployment. Those who opposed it said it would cause inflation, or that we had **enough** leisure.

The Federal Minister for Customs has **banned a US film from release in Australia**. Its name is *Skyjacked* and tells the story of a plane hijacking in the air by a US sergeant....

The Minister said that his reason was that experience had shown that **copycat crimes often follow on** from viewing such films. "This type of film would have an influence on a deranged mind."

Governments in several jurisdictions are about to **control the dumping of waste material in the sea** around Australia. Materials to be banned include cyanide, explosives, ammunition, pesticidal poison and lead sludge...

Previously, waste material could be dumped freely or under Licence. The ban will basically be effective for the entire Continental Shelf....

In NSW, in the last few years, the Government avoided sea dumping by **the provision of a sealed bunker in the Western regions of NSW**.

BLACK POWER IN OZ?

In the US, Black Power was at its peak. Its purpose was to build on a world-wide movement that opposed the dominance of the white man. Some years earlier, it had been using peaceful methods for change but in the last few years, it had changed to violence. A series of murders of public officials, and explosions of bombs shocked America. The big question here was, would it spread to Australia?

The burning issue for our Aborigines was their land rights claims over property across the nation. In 1972, four Aborigines set a number of tents, along with road signs on lawns, close to the Old Parliament House. After six months, the "tent embassy" was removed by police, and over the years that followed, it came and went.

It looked scraggy, and was no advertisement for the Capitol of the nation as world leaders and diplomats visited our seat of Government. Overall though, it was only that - an eye-sore. It did have some effect because disputes, over whether it should stay or go, kept the various claims of Aboriginal people in the minds of many people, and engendered sympathy for their cause.

The police actions to shut down the Embassy stirred some passions among writers.

Letters, (Rev) B Wilson, Anglican Chaplain, University of NSW. My small son (4 1/2) looked at the front page of Friday's "Herald" and asked me to explain the pictures printed there. They showed the struggle between

Commonwealth police and members of the Aboriginal "embassy."

I explained that the Aborigines were sad because they were treated badly by the white men who had come to live in their country. I told him that some Aborigines had put up a tent outside the building where the men who run our country worked so that they would be reminded to help the Aboriginal people.

My son asked: "Why are the men in police helmets fighting them?" I explained that they were policemen who had been sent to make the Aborigines go away. He then said: "Policemen are supposed to catch bad men - why are they fighting Aborigines?"

Out of the mouths of babes and sucklings indeed!

Letters, T Whelan. The Aborigines have at least won the battle, if not the war. Canberra has now unequivocally affirmed its recognition of the Aboriginal's application for membership in the Power Politics Club of Australia.

Now that the Government admits that the Aborigines are a viable political force, perhaps their rights will be protected after all. Or must we coerce them into using more potent political power than non-violence?

Letters, G Noon, R Jamieson. We would like to express our disgust at the actions of the Australian Government in provoking the incident at the Aboriginal "embassy" on Thursday and later attempting to "whitewash" its actions.

A clearer demonstration of our lack of sensitivity and gross stupidity could not be envisaged.

Letters, D Daintree, Chairman, University of New England, Liberal Club. I would like to join all those who have expressed their anger and disgust at the suppression of the Aboriginal "embassy" in Canberra.

The "embassy" stood on the lawns opposite Parliament House for six months, and the sincerity, fortitude and restraint of those associated with it was, if I may say so without sounding patronising, a credit to the honour of the Aboriginal race.

By contrast, the arrogance and ruthlessness of the authorities who planned its removal and the indecent haste with which they accomplished their design must be a source of shame to all Australians. Could the Government not have offered even one block of land, with diplomatic privileges, as compensation to a people who have been deprived of almost all the land they ever possessed?

The Government's inept and tactless handling of this affair will win widespread support for the cause of Aboriginal land rights and, tragically, will further alienate and strengthen that small but increasing element in the Aboriginal population which sees violence as the only remaining means of regaining the dignity of its race.

Comment. All of these, and others, were not happy with the closure. But some writers saw it from a different point of view.

Letters, Hugh Ryan. I do not like the sight of the Aboriginal Embassy, and I worry about the sanitation there.

But these are trivial matters. Of more concern is the message it gives that it is proper that Aborigines can set up on Commonwealth land, at any place, and any time, for whatever purpose, and be allowed to do that.

And I worry about whether it can be done with State land, or Council land, or even sporting fields. In a society that is bending over backwards to be nice to Aborigines, anything is possible.

Comment. Mr Ryan was at least right in one respect. Seven other Embassies did set up in various places, for varying durations.

Did a version of America's Black Power come to Australia? Not at all. Apart from a few punch-ups here and there with the cops at demos, the most exciting event was this Aboriginal Embassy.

DECIMALISATION

A few years ago, the entire nation changed over to decimal currency. We learned to talk and think in terms of dollars and cents in stead of pounds, shillings and pence. The changeover was hard for most people and, by 1972, many people still had not conquered the conversion.

Now the day was nigh when other units were due to change over. This was shaping up to be a bigger battle than that for currency.

Letters, P Lovett. It is to be hoped that the details of metric conversion are not left entirely to academics who adopt the attitude that the conversion must be "all the way." Why change to kilometres? Why depart from Fahrenheit?

Obviously, considerable advantages will be apparent in the long run by adopting certain aspects of the metric system. However, for example, there is absolutely no advantage whatsoever in adopting kilometres to replace miles. Instead of 1,760 yards to the mile, this merely changes to 1,609 metres to the mile. So let us retain the mile, as we obviously will be retaining the knot (the international measurement of speed-miles per hour for aircraft and shipping).

The very considerable cost of changing all signposts, maps, charts and speedometers will be avoided. Why, then, do the academics consider the change necessary? The USA has no inclination of changing to kilometres.

In respect of temperature readings, there are actual disadvantages in changing to centigrade due to its compressed scale.

The academic approach should be tempered by practicable considerations. Let us adopt the metric system where it is of advantage. Otherwise, let us retain present measurements.

There were a lot of units involved. Take the case of ordinary eggs. They became a matter of some controversy. **In viewing this**, there is no need for you to follow the argument. You should just look at the complications that humble eggs cause.

Letters, R Roberts. I would like to draw to your attention a blatant piece of metric conversion profiteering by a Government-sponsored agency.

Until this week, hen eggs in NSW were in 18oz, 21oz and 24oz per dozen sizes. They now come in 720g, 660g, 600g and 540g sizes, with the last three selling at the previous 24oz, 21oz and 18oz prices.

What is not said is that 660g is only 23oz. Admittedly 600g is 21oz and 540g is 19oz, but with the closer spacing of the grade sizes plus the addition of the 620g per dozen size, there is no doubt that the consumer is once again suffering.

Is anyone benefiting? Presumably the producers aren't.

Comment. Some people thought that Centigrade would be better than Fahrenheit, and hoped the Weather Bureau would change over soon. Others wanted the freezing point of water to become officially 0 degrees Centigrade.

Others asked what was the utility in recording nautical speed in knots when most distances would be measured in kilometres. Others wondered about the economics of changes at all when half the world would be required to change over to a new system.

And what about America? It was not going to change over from miles and yards to kilometres?

Letters, D Allen. In reference to the Letters from G Brown and V Collins objecting to aspects of change in the metric system, I am tempted to ask what was their attitude to the introduction of decimal currency.

I wonder how many people who objected to that change in 1966 could sustain their objections in 1972. Perhaps those who did would still want us all to return to the system of pounds, shillings and pence. I doubt if they would receive much support.

Comment. I think that Mr Allen underestimates the trouble that some people have with their money under the new system. Still, we will probably never know.

Also mentioned were volumes. Were we Australians to change from gills, pints, quarts, gallons to litres? Could we change from asking how many miles to the gallon? It's hard enough to work in a single variable, but much harder when you have a ratio with two variables.

So the arguments rolled on.

But of course, you all know the result by the 2020's. We are all reasonably familiar with our current weights, and measures, and distances, and temperatures. But I still measure the distance between Town A and Town B in miles, I do a quick mental conversion in my head when the distance in kilometres is mentioned.

I still measure land area in acres, my height is still in inches, my weight is in pounds. I travel at 60 miles an hour. I want to buy half a pound of grapes.

I suppose that all you younger kids outshine me and measure the count of silly old buggers in dinosaurs.

Question. If you bought two ounces of Log Cabin, how many smokes would you get from that?

TOOTHPICKS IN THE NEWS

Letters, J Bretnall. A portentous Customs Department ruling has come down on the all-important subject of toothpicks. As from July 13, only toothpicks made from white birchwood will be imported free of duty. All other wooden toothpicks will pay 30 per cent Customs duty, or 20 per cent under the preferential rate.

Can we afford to pay someone to create such a pettifogging ruling? Are such trivialities worthy of such complexity? May the Lord help us.

RHODESIANS DECLARED BLACK

The Olympic Games for 1972 are just around the corner. But they have hit a hurdle. Black athletes from mainly African nations, and the United States, have said that they will not compete if the team from Rhodesia is allowed to enter.

Their claim is that there was a bias against blacks in picking the team there, and because the blacks generally were not being given a fair go in their everyday lives.

Of course, this was a time when blacks around the world were fighting to get rid of the colonial status that had frustrated their claims for self determination for years, especially obvious since WWII.

But it was the first time that nations had deliberately introduced world politics into the Games.

The matter of Rhodesia was resolved quickly and ruthlessly. The IOC met a few times in two days, and decided that the Games could not be held if so many of its best athletes were not competing, so the invitation to Rhodesia to attend was withdrawn.

This made no difference to the Games, but it left a lot of people wondering what could be done against such an obvious case of blackmail.

A BIT OF A RAMBLE ON TROUSSEAUS

Occasionally, near the end of a book, I indulge myself a little, with a few paragraphs on some small, inconsequential thing that comes into my mind. In the next section, I have done that.

Does any other oldie remember what **a trousseau** was? Or a glory box? Or a dowry box? It was a collection of linen and cotton household goods that would be useful to a newly-married girl as she moved into her own home. Items such as sheets and blankets, table cloths, quilts, and covers. Also household goods in more modern times, such as irons, toasters, and even electric jugs.

Generally, they were accumulated by parents for a girl once she got a suitor, and were handed over about the time of the marriage. Most most girls, in 1940 say, were given a trousseau at the appropriate stage.

But they have died out now. By 1970, they seem to have disappeared off the face of this part of the planet.

A couple of lifelong friends, both clergymen, told me that about 2010, the **practice of giving to** their children had given way to having very expensive weddings. To girls in particular, they want to give her the wedding of her dreams.

But they went on to say that by 2020, this trend, still growing, was supplemented by the gift of a lump of money to buy a new dwelling for themselves.

Comment. Some things never change. But in the world of wedding presents a lot has changed in a century.

As a side issue, I point out that all of the above highlights **how much richer the population has become** in that period. **Here.**

SEPTEMBER NEWS ITEMS

I have to warn you. **The 1972 Olympic Games opened in Munich.** No matter how I try, it is certain that a few items will cloud these pages. I apologise and am determined to keep them to a minimum.

The High Court has decided that **18-year-olds cannot vote in the upcoming Federal elections**. But it added that the Government could change the law if it chose....

PM Menzies says he will not change in time for this year's vote, but might do it later....

Note that youngsters do have the right to vote in Western Australia and South Australia, but **only for State elections**.

In NSW, it is easier to buy gelignite, up to 25 pounds, than it is to buy fire crackers. The latter are very restricted, but the gelignite buyer must only supply his name and address....

In the last eight months, the Army has been called on to remove 894 sticks from their premises by citizens who had grown wary of them.

On September 4th, five Arabs broke into the German village for athletes at the Olympic Games, and **shot and killed two Officials**. They are also holding 13 athletes as hostages for the release of Arab prisoners elsewhere....

The Games were halted for a day.

The hype for the coming Federal elections, in about three months, is now starting. Gough Whitlam got off to an early start at a rally and said that **Labor would win an extra 18 seats**. That's a lot of seats. Can the Liberals go even higher?

September 6th. **Arab terrorists attacked the Israeli Olympic team** as it alighted from a plane near Munich. **17 Israeli athletes were killed, and three Arabs, and one policeman....**

A full-scale battle ensued using machine guns, three helicopters were destroyed, 20 grenades were exploded, and 300 passengers were trapped inside the terminal as the battle went on outside....

All the hostages from the previous day were slaughtered....

The Games were again postponed for a day. The Israeli team has withdrawn from the Games.

57 police officers in NSW have been dismissed so far this year for breaches of regulations and discipline.

The seven biggest banks in Australia have announced that **they** plan to implement a scheme whereby **customers can use a "credit card" to buy goods** without a cash payment....

This is the first group to make the service open to all comers, rather than to just their own customers....

The US claims that the model is working well. There are many here who say that it will collapse. **They will never have faith in the cashless society....**

What do you think?

Back to the Credit Card scheme. Three days after its announcement, the Consumers Association said it **would not participate because it would bring higher prices and taxes**.

The Games are back again. Two successful American athletes were banned from future events and future Games after they talked through their award ceremony, **gave a clench fist to the crowd** and, in explanation, were defiant.

September 11th. **The Israeli air force has bombed Syria** on two days as retaliation for the Munich massacre....

The UN has called a special Council meeting on the matter, and this will do nothing, as usual.

A Brisbane woman was the first person in the nation to go to the Supreme Court using **a do-it-yourself kit for divorce**. The kit was created by the Queensland Divorce Law Reform Association. The woman said her divorce would cost her $32. Most similar cases, with the help of the legal profession, would cost about $450....

The number of divorces in Australia was rising. This was a good time to market a do-it-yourself kit.

Bathurst Council in NSW will ask smokers to **give up smoking for February** next year and donate the money they saved to a Council Fund.

THE GUILT OF WORKING MOTHERS

There were many women who took the view that women who went back to work after having a child were "Guilty". No matter what the circumstances, they were wrong to do so.

Some of the women who said this based their criticism on whatever part of the Bible they found convenient. Others based their opinion on the belief that children suffered if they were not with their mother for every minute of their first five years.

Many others took a different view. Some said, almost facetiously, that offices were becoming air-conditioned, or that it was for the money and survival, or that it was for romance and mating.

More seriously one mother said that we work to withstand the pressures of inflation and the rapacious demands of a consumer society.

But whenever mothers went back to work, they faced the charge that they were somehow guilty or if they did not feel guilty, they were nagged by the thought that they were not doing the right thing. The woman below, mother of a five-year old and a six-year old, expresses herself clearly.

Letters, Dot Martin. Am I guilty because I leave my two children at home with my parents for two hours on schools day? No, not at all.

Do I feel guilty because I cannot be with them in the ten weeks a year of school holidays? No.

Because I negotiated the time off from work in those periods.

Do I feel guilty because some few days I am very tired when I get home, and take the lazy way out with preparing a three-course meal? No. Because kids have to live in the real world, and baked beans once a week will not hurt them.

There are other occasions where I do not do a perfect job. My family knows that a bed of roses should not be their expectations, and they roll with it. And in fact, if they have a loving home and loving parents, they do not even notice it.

Occasionally, rarely, I kick myself because I miss out on an event because I am working. But that to is part of lie. If that's the worst that happens to a family, then theirs is a happy life.

So, no. I do not feel the least bit guilty.

Letters, Phil Bourke. I appreciated Dot Martin's Letter. Though I do have a few thoughts to add.

Dot appears to have good, balanced family. In fact, most families are like that. But there are others who do not.

These mothers and fathers, and their children, have to scrape every penny to keep a roof over their heads. They cannot make the arrangements that Dot does. And some of these then go to work. Should they feel guilty?

In my opinion, not at all,   Think of the consequences if they did not. Then there would be no roof. No, these people are guilt free.

Then there are others who go to work because they want to. I suppose this brings me back to Dot's case. Except for the fact that it is personal desire that motivates them. Should they feel guilty? Not at all, Any person who does what they want, and can make it happen, should feel care-free in this respect, and go guilt-less.

The people whom I have left out, the ones who want to work and can't make it happen, they might feel bad about it, but clearly have no guilt about working when they can.

So, women of the world, do your job, or do not do your job, but never feel guilty at all about any of it.

Comment. These nice words from two writers were not exactly matched by other writers.

Letters, (Dr) P Cook, ANZ College of Psychiatrists. "Some mothers must work because they need the money. The Government, for reasons of economic policy, wish to see more women working. But, to work full time, a mother must expect that her child will attend nursery for extended hours and during school holidays.

Our evidence is, however, that it is generally undesirable, except to prevent a greater evil, to separate mother and child for a whole day in the nursery."

The need for children aged three to five to have some part-time kindergarten experience is a quite different matter, and the two subjects should not be confused under the issue of pre-school education.

Letters, S Lewis. Recently I advertised in the local paper for a woman to look after my baby for one day a week. I had 40 replies.

Money-grubbing women? Or just plain bored and lonely women?

Comment. I hardly need to mention how much the scene has changed by the 2020's. The industry has moved from a backyard existence staffed by part-timers, often unpaid, in spare rooms in a house. It is now doing quite well as specialised playschools, with trained and certified staff, with wages set by the government. All sorts of regulations govern the standard of the education offered, and a big part of their money comes from the government.

The number of children at pre-school has grown at a fantastic rate. Children who attend pre-school are no longer the exception. And the proportion of mothers who are working has grown at the same rate.

That, of course, has stopped that particular debate about guilt. Clearly now there is no argument about guilt for the mums who want to work. In fact, most of their life-styles are built on the expectation that mothers will bring in a certain of money each week.

Guilt has gone. We now have the right balance.

Or do we? I expect that we will never really know.

MY INDIFFERENCE TO THE GAMES

I would like to point out to you why I appear cold to the Games. It is not that I do not like them. I enjoy watching any sport when talented, highly-trained determined athletes combine to put on a spectacle. I like Rugby League, tennis, golf, womens volleyball, boxing. It's great to watch them and to savour them in conversation.

But the 1972 Games started to disillusion me. We read about two incidents, and there were more, when politics intervened into the world of sports. The first was the ejection of the Rhodesian team. The second was the massacre of the Israeli team because of a hatred that has been going on for centuries. Both of these offend me, to see sport used in this way.

But beyond that, I was further soured at the next Games by the entry of the national spin-makers who used every win to crow about their superiority over other countries. It started in 1976, just in a small way, but it grew, and is still growing, so that every win for a most courageous and talented athlete is now recorded, in all media, as a victory for one particular **nation**. The headlines, during the most recent Games, have been not what a great performer some athlete is, but what is the national medal count.

Let me spell it out. The more medals you can brag about, the higher up the ladder you are in world esteem. What a cheap sense of values is now driving the Games.

So, my friends, with these surprisingly cross words, I hope you will excuse me for being not so happy with the Olympics. I might do better next time,

OZ REACTION TO MUNICH

The *SMH* captured the horror felt by Australians to the massacre.

Editorial. Political quarrels and murderous hatreds intrude, culminating in a frightful episode which has shocked the world and tarnished the lustre of its greatest sporting gathering. Mindless, irrational violence would be horrifying enough; but the slaughter at Munich was an example of something far more dreadful which is becoming alarmingly widespread - the use of terrorism as a deliberate instrument of policy. The Arabs responsible for this tragedy were, like the IRA gunmen in Ulster, seeking to achieve by terror and intimidation what they were too weak to achieve by open force of arms.

THE NATION'S HEALTH

In 1972, Australia saw itself as a nation that was physically fit. Our attitude was that we had the weather, and the space, to allow us to play sport and be active at any time. We had little of the extreme heat and extreme cold that other countries lived in misery with.

So, we had built a legend of ourselves as a nation of the great outdoors, of sun-bronzed cricketers wrangling untamed sheep in the foothills of the Blue Mountains, while drinking lots of beer out of empty oyster shells.

Or something like that.

But, despite the lovely legend, we were fast losing our physical fitness. That is, according to the Professor below.

Letters, J Bloomfield, University of WA. I strongly support the recent proposal of Mr B Cohen, MP, to the Australian Labor Party Caucus regarding the establishment of a ministry of sport by the Federal Government.

There are some critics who will maintain that such a government body is not warranted and that Australians are a sport-loving (to be distinguished from sport-participating), fit and healthy people. Statistics gathered over the past 20 years, however, show that our general present day level of physical fitness is gradually declining.

At the present time in this country 55 per cent of deaths are due to cardiovascular disease, and Australia now has the third highest incidence of this degenerative disease in the world. Perhaps the most alarming fact is that the increase of cardiovascular disease is most marked in young and middle-aged men.

It is also interesting to note that the rejection rate of young men called up for national service is now up to 48 per cent, and the life expectancy for males is currently less in Australia than in Europe (longevity being 67.9

years for the Australian male in comparison with 70.5 years for his European counterpart). Moreover, whereas life expectancy is increasing in Europe it is diminishing slightly in Australia.

Finally, when one compares the results of the few valid physical fitness tests which have been carried out in Australia with European results, even our children do not compare well. None of these facts, taken individually, is perhaps highly significant, but when grouped together they show a dangerous trend which is greatly concerning the medical and physical education professions in Australia.

The above problems have mainly occurred because of increasing urbanisation and the automation of our daily existence. Man, in changing his physical world to meet the needs of an urban society, has interfered with his biological adaptation, which was achieved through a very long process of natural evolution. Previously man has been forced to have physical activity to stay alive; in our present living situation, an unnatural one for a body which is biochemically animal, artificial means must be created to again involve man in physical activity. More than 20 European countries, and several on other continents, now have ministries of recreation and sport.

Comment. This was a view that was generally resisted for decades and even now, in the 2020's. Only in the last decade have we started to accept that in the cities we no longer had the time, and the space, to be active when we wanted. Sporting Clubs have taken over from kids playing on streets and in paddocks, TV has kept all of us enthralled in the evenings, everyone rides in a car rather than walk. Yoga is now the rage, and Saturday night dancing has disappeared. You get my meaning.

Nowadays there are many who are trumpeting the same message as Professor Bloomfield. But 50 years earlier, his voice was a lonely one.

GAMES FINISHED ON SEPTEMBER 12

The Olympic Games finished without the normal fanfare. This was obviously because of the effect of the massacre.

But even in their dying minutes, the sensations kept coming. The Pakistan hockey team, after losing the final, refused to take part in the medal presentation ceremony. **The eleven players in the team were banned for life amid a lot of scuffling.**

In all, no one had any cause for satisfaction from the many disruptive events of this set of Olympics. Apart from the obvious tragedies, there was incident after incident in which the athletes deliberately disrupted the events and their aftermath.

Many commentators wondered publicly whether the Games should be somehow diminished in scope, or even if they should be abandoned entirely in future.

OCTOBER NEWS ITEMS

October 7th. Six girls and their teacher were kidnapped from a small school 40 miles from Melbourne. A note was left demanding one million Dollars for their release....

There are only eight students at the school. Two of them were away sick....

October 8th. The young teacher and the six girls, who had been imprisoned in a van, kicked the door in, and escaped. This was about dawn. They scrambled round for an hour in the bushland, and eventually found four adults who were there to shoot rabbits....

Police are searching for the two kidnappers.

Princess Margaret and Lord Snowden arrived in Perth at **the start of a Royal Tour**....

Comment. Australia still loved the British Royal Family. Republicanism was still a long way off. Though it was true to say, there was a small stirring for it in a few breasts.

October 10th. Two men were charged in Melbourne over the kidnapping. Each faced seven charges.

Just a reminder that **the war in Vietnam was still going on.** And so too were the Paris Peace talks that were hoping to come to a ceasefire agreement....

Some commentators were hoping that Nixon would be keen to settle so that he could bring this good news just prior to **next month's US elections.**

The day of the election here has been set for December 2nd. Now the battle will really start.

At long last, the Government has announced that **FM radio will be heard across the nation**. The first stations will begin to broadcast in three years, and will start with the bigger cities and gradually be extended....

FM radio has been working overseas for many years. **It was first used in the US in 1940.**

The recently deceased Poet Laureate was Cecil Day Lewis. His successor will be Sir John Betjeman....

London, Buckingham Palace. You will doubtless be familiar with what a Poet Laureate does, so I will just point out that his salary will be $142 a year, **plus $27 in lieu of a butt of sack**.

Lord Snowden in Perth Hospital brought joy to two patients by allowing them to kiss him on the cheek....

Quote from newspaper: Young pantry-maid Julie **(yellow dressing gown, broken leg)** said she had kissed him too, and it was quite a privilege.

The Government will introduce laws that will impose **life sentences for hijacking aeroplanes.** Pressure had been building from pilots' associations to have this done. Several strikes threatened by pilots will now be mothballed.

WEEKEND SPORT FOR CHILDREN

For over a year, questions have been raised about the value of sport at the weekend for children. Three major sports, Rugby League, Soccer, and Rugby Union, have been discussing among themselves whether to fully drop their programmes for juniors. All three involve heavy body contact, with Rugby League being the toughest.

Those arguing against continuing say that immature bodies cannot withstand the brutal shocks that they get, without some immediate or longer-term damage.

They also say that the adulation showered on "stars" by parents is not good for the children. "Some of the youngsters appear to be brainwashed by their parents into a code of brutality. Going out and having a run has disappeared. Egged on by their parents, they are callous towards their opposition, and will do anything to win. This is not sport, this is winning at all cost....

"They also argue that the boys are burned out by age 14. They are tired of the games, and no longer look forward to their matches, and front only to give satisfaction to their parents."

The most widely affected sport is Rugby League, with its greater violence. And it is taking the lead in looking at proposals to cut weekend junior play. It has formed various Committees to look at proposals for bans....

Currently, if all three sports implemented the bans, it would mean at least 30,000 youngsters would miss out on Saturday sport until they reached 14 years of age.

Comment. It seemed unlikely at the time. After half a dozen years of discussion, all talk died away.

PUNISHMENT FITTING THE CRIME

Letters, D H Brown and 36 others. We were disappointed to note that the market gardener who dragged a dog behind the back of his car at speeds of up to 40 mph until it died shortly thereafter had his sentence reduced from one month's jail to a fine of $300 upon appeal.

We also noted that the two men who damaged football posts during a recent Rubgy tour received fines of $500 each and good behaviour bonds as well as being required to pay for the damage of the football posts.

To our minds there seems to be a substantial inequity in the punishment of these two offences, and we feel that the $300 fine for deliberate torture inflicted upon an animal is a sorry reflection on the quality of justice in the State of New South Wales.

THE 35-HOUR WEEK AND THE ELECTIONS

The Prime Minister announced that there should be no more 35-hour working-week judgements at the moment. And he indicated that this decision could stand for a while . He and the Liberal Party had been against it from the time it was first mentioned.

This was clearly the beginning of an election strategy. He could see that most of **his faithful** were opposed to the introduction of the reduced working week, and was in the process of making it a major plank in his platform.

The Labor Opposition, under Whitlam, had not revealed any of its policies yet, but there was no doubt that they would fight in favour of the reduction.

It is shaping as the most interesting election in years.

KOOKAS AND KANGAS

Letters, G Curran. I wonder if some of your erudite readers could help me? A current writing assignment makes it necessary that I track down the meaning of the words kookaburra and kangaroo.

Various impressive authorities have failed to come up with satisfactory answers. Kookaburra could be derived from the sound the bird makes, but I'm not wholly convinced.

As for kangaroo, I seem to recall reading (or perhaps I made it up) that Captain Cook, on seeing one of these strange animals for the first time, asked a conveniently handy Aboriginal what it was. The man replied, "Kangaroo," which meant, "I don't know."

The good captain assumed that the native was giving the creature's name, so the first historic communication breakdown between white and black on Australian soil gave us our label for one of the land's most famous animals ... but, of course, that's not true - is it?

Letters, C Keese. G Curran was partly right about Captain Cook's question and the Aboriginal's answer.

The native was, in fact, giving the captain the actual name of the marsupial.

I was stationed in the area occupied by this particular tribe for 10 years back in the thirties and heard the name used many times by the tribal Aborigines.

WOOL MARKETING

I am getting close to the end of this book and have given little attention to news and thoughts from the country. So, I want to fix that now. Fortunately, there is one such interesting story ready and willing to be told right now.

We all know that for a few years in the Korean War, Australia again rode on the sheeps' back. Soldiers in freezing Korea needed to be kept alive with lots of woolen clothing, and hence the price of wool, on the open market, reached record highs.

Since then, synthetics have eaten into the market for wool, and at the same time the Vietnam War came and has almost gone. But the demand for woolen clothes in tropical Vietnam did not see too much increase in prices.

But now, in wool markets all over Australia, wool prices have shot up. Day after day, the prices rise and then rise until once again, new records are being set. "Bales that would have sold for 40 cents a few years ago are now selling for 400", "all through the Bathurst region, wool growers are drinking champagne and some are giving it to their sheep."

No one is quite sure of why this is happening. They know that frenzied buyers are mainly Japanese. But why this sudden demand? It could be that their involvement with fabric made from the finest of wools is fitting in with new fashions in Japan, but is this enough reason for a huge surge?

One grazier has a suggestion.

Letters, R Smith. The fantastic increase in wool prices over the past two weeks has given rise to many and varied interpretations of why this spectacular improvement has taken place.

One reason put forward has been "panic" buying on the part of several large operators, based on the premise that a considerable amount of wool has been sold privately in the shed and on the sheep's back. Indeed, there are some who declare that by Christmas most of this year's production will have been sold in some form or other.

The incidence of private buying has increased over the past two years in the eastern States for a variety of reasons, not the least of which has been cash in the hand soon after delivery.

The decision by several brokers to move away from traditional auction selling to include private selling, sale by tender and sale of wool on the sheep's back has indeed created confusion in the minds of many producers. Private buyers have been stomping the countryside, with the result that certain **wool destined for auction has been sold at the farm gate**. The upshot of all this has been the worst kind of disorderly marketing I have ever experienced.

Nobody really knows how much wool has already been sold, or indeed how much wool has been sold by growers for delivery over the next few months. No wonder there is chaos and fear over future quantities for this season.

In order to allay the obvious concern of our overseas customers about production this season, the Wool Commission must do everything it can to ascertain the quantity of wool already sold privately and through auction, the number of bales contracted for future delivery from farms, and endeavour to give an indication of likely quantities available for the remainder of this season.

Naturally this will be difficult, but it must be attempted.

Finally, the sooner we return to the orderly marketing of the Australian wool clip by controlling private selling the sooner we will create the type of stability which, I am sure, the majority of the wool industry is seeking.

Comment. Mr Smith's Letter required serious thought. But it was rejected basically because such a process would be seen as **a constraint on trade**. In later years, various Wool Marketing Schemes and bodies were proposed.

So that it came closer to the idea that a Commission should in effect buy the entire Australian clip and stockpile or sell it, according to local supply, world demand, and likely price

LIFE IN THE BIG APPLE

New York, New York, it's a wonderful town, we have been told for decades. And glitzy images, of Tiffany's, and Broadway, and Sachs 5th Avenue, are known worldwide. But in 1972, the realities of life in New York were being revealed.

A nasty report of the ongoing travails of children and parents was released. It showed that half of the 300,000 High school students take drugs. Twenty per cent of Juniors were also using. These figures do not include hard-cores who had prematurely left school because of drugs or expulsions.

The Study, conducted by a Commission appointed by Governor Rockefeller, also recommended that more security guards, to combat violence and drugs, be employed. In 1972!

It also approved of more routine medical examinations of High Schoolers to fight the spread of venereal disease.

ABORIGINES

A number of Governmental moves in the last ten years have improved the lot and the status of Aborigines. And social acceptance has increased a great deal at the same time.

But below is an example of how much more needs to be done.

Letters, (Mrs) F Bandler, Aborigines and Torres Strait Islanders. The news that a Queensland Aboriginal stockman, Mr John Belia, has **gained in court the right to use his own wages has opened doors for thousands of other Aboriginal workers to do the same thing**.

It has been the work of the Federal Council for the Advancement of Aborigines and Torres Strait Islanders to enable black people in Australia to win greater economic and political freedom. It was also in this case. The council has been working on this legal case for over a year.

The Council was responsible for the referendum of 1967, which means that there are now Federal grants taking the place of humiliating charity for Aboriginal education and welfare.

We are a voluntary organisation, 17 years in the field on a national scale, a non-government body without a Government subsidy. Our activity concerns the equality and freedom from controls that should be open to Aborigines and

Islanders, as they are to other Australians - in a single word, independence.

Comment. In case you do not know, prior to this, Mr Belia would have handed his wages to a manager, who would have released them at his caprice over time. This was because some Aborigines were deemed to be unable to spend their own money wisely.

PARACHUTING GIRL DIES

A girl, aged 19, was dropped from a plane in a parachute near Camden in Sydney. Her fall was routine until a gust of wind took her a mile from the landing zone.

She landed in a large dam, and by the time rescuers arrived, she had drowned.

ARE CHRISTIAN CHURCHES DYING?

Since the end of WWII, there is no doubt that the influence of the Christian Churches has declined. You can see it in the drop in the numbers attending church on Sundays, in a fall in the number of clergymen dropping in at home for a chat, in the lack of newspaper coverage for Sunday sermons, and in all sorts of matters.

Towards the end of October, one clergyman did speak up in public about this. He was the chaplain at Sydney University Wesley College, and was not without supporters. Though he was regarded by many as a wild cannon, and certainly his views on a lot of matters did not represent most of his faith.

In any case, at a church conference, he argued that the influence of the Christian Church was waning. He said that the Churches were at their geriatric stage, he talked about outmoded world views, and specifically that the Churches were dying.

He went on to say that **the good Christian values that they promoted were here to stay. But the Churches were failing in their attempts to champion them**. The promotion of such values was coming from the laity, not from the clergy.

These views were not at all revolutionary. But what was striking was that they were given such public prominence in a clerical world that was most reluctant to speak them

Comment. By the Twenties, such views are common, and acknowledged by most clergy. But to hear them uttered in public, and in such an open forum, came as quite a shock to church observers.

NOVEMBER NEWS ITEMS

Rudolf Nureyev arrived in Sydney. He will film his own version of *Don Quixote* with the Australian Ballet.

A woman living in the outskirts of Sydney **left her sleeping daughter in a car** in a shopping centre. She went to buy articles and **was away for "just" ten minutes.** On return, the car, with the baby inside, had been stolen. Police were called and a search begun....

A few hours later, a factory worker happened to go into the long grass behind the factory, and heard a baby crying. It was the kidnapped baby....

It seems likely that the baby would have been there all weekend if the worker had not gone by chance into the grass. The driver of the car had not yet been found.

Comment. By now, in the 2020's, no one would think of leaving a baby in a car for 10 minutes..

The Builders Labourers Federation, **led by Jack Mundy,** is having trouble with the NSW Government. And vice versa....

There is a lot of talk that the BLF Green strikes, and associated violence, will cause deaths. Jack Mundy is intent on suing Premier Askin, dozens of allegations of bashings of dissenting workers are being touted, and violence on their building sites is forcing some construction companies out of business.

Comment. I happen to know that next year, and beyond, there will be a lot more action to come.

Richard Nixon won the 1972 election for President for the next four years. He took 49 of the 50 States, and his popular vote was 44 million to 27 million. **It was a landslide.** Looks like Nixon will have a trouble-free four more years.

There are some bitter feeling in the NSW coalfields. The pendulum has now swung wildly, and supply is starting to outstrip demand. ....

So various authorities are demanding **that some mines cease production or close shop altogether.** And miners there are going on strike in order to resist the cuts. Not much logic here, but that's the way the coal mining industry has always worked. If you have a problem, any problem, call a strike.

The Melbourne Cup was won by outsider *Piping Lane* at 40-1. Bookmakers said it was almost a skinner for the books.

The Vietnam War is almost over. All of our troops have returned to Australia. Draft Peace Treaties, between everyone and his dogs, are everywhere. There is a lot of talk that the conscription of our young men will stop before the end of the year....

But the law of the land still stands. Young 20-year-old men will still be liable to be conscripted, and spending two years of **their** lives in the military.

14,000 Catholic priests worldwide applied to leave the clergy last year. More evidence of **the declining influence of the Churches.**

THE COMING ELECTION

It's time to look at the upcoming Federal Elections in more detail. As you all know, we have two main political Parties, and each has a leader whose performance is very important to the outcome. The incumbent Government was under the control of the Liberal Party, the Party of big business. Its leader was William McMahon, from Sydney's Eastern suburbs, and he exemplifies all the wealth and power that came from that region.

He had only held the position of Prime Minister for about two years, and he gave the impression that he wanted the job, but he wanted to keep the job in perspective, with none of obsession that compelled the Opposition Leader, Gough Whitlam.

McMahon was saddled with a Party not fully convinced that he was the right man for the job. When he was elected to the Leadership, it was by only one vote, **that of his opponent, John Gorton**. In terms of public appeal, he was not at all popular. Many voters saw him as aloof, secluded in the Eastern Suburbs, and remote from the problems of the common man.

Whitlam, the current Opposition Leader was a different proposition. Great speaker, very vital, he could be smooth, but he had a gift for the common argot. His policies were well thought out, and manipulated so that he would appeal to large groups of people. Such as hospital patients, public servants and women. Soft targets, but Boy, do they count.

From every perspective, it seemed at the moment that Labor would shoe it in. All the polls showed that Whitlam as a Leader would win easily, and that his Party behind him would win a clear majority of seats.

If all that happened, then the next few years would be very exciting, because the policies Whitlam proposed were due to affect the population down to the last person.

The Australian elections will be held on Saturday, December 2nd. All eligible persons must vote.

PROGRAMME NOTE

For the remainder of this Chapter, I will focus on election matters. I will make no attempt to strike a balance between the two Parties, but because most of my material comes from the *SMH*, so too will be my coverage. I assure you that if Labor still published its *Labour Daily*, my efforts would give them equal time. So my quotes will reflect a generous Liberal bias, but I hope I leave you with the feeling that I am being as even-handed as I can be.

HATCHET JOB ON LABOR BY THE *SMH*

SMH Editorial and other Editors nation-wide:

Labor was rejected in 1949 because it was wedded to a wartime network of authoritarian bureaucratic controls and because it attempted, without a mandate, to nationalise the private banking system.

It was rejected in the 1950s again because of its authoritarian record, then because Dr Evatt tried to buy votes with a fantastic, uncosted welfare program at a time of surging individual enterprise, and, finally, because it split into irreconcilable factions.

It did have bad luck not to win power early in the 1960s when the Menzies Government deserved censure for inept economic policies. But it later forfeited that moment of credibility by once again falling into factionalism, emphasising its subservience to the trade-unions, and, above all, embracing foreign and defence policies which unashamedly reflected the neutralist and isolationist compulsions of its Left Wing.

What of substance has Labor offered in this campaign to convert mistrust into trust? Under its reformed but more centralised and even more powerful federal executive, it is more than ever subservient to the special interests and capricious impulses of the trade-unions.

It still seeks to dazzle voters with a far-flung galaxy of mainly uncosted or uncostable promises. It relies for their implementation on an expanded bureaucracy, bolstered this time by a meritocracy of putative wise men and working under a brazenly centralist and authoritarian Government.

It still plans to pursue isolationist and neutralist foreign and defence policies which will cut the size of our armed forces by more than half and confine them behind or around our shoreline, and which must imperil the trust we have earned among our neighbours and with our powerful allies.

Comment. The *SMH* clearly does not think much of the Labor Party's past performance, nor of its likely future prospects. I expect the *Labour Daily* could do an equally good job on the Liberals.

A FEW OPINIONS ON THE ELECTIONS

Letters, Eric Willis, NSW Minister for Education. Your editorial "Behind Labor" is indeed timely. It draws attention to the fact that irrespective of the personal qualities of the candidates chosen by the people next Saturday, a Labor Government, if elected, **would not necessarily be controlled by those parliamentary representatives**.

Such a Government would be largely controlled by the still **"faceless" men** of the ALP Federal Executive.

Letters, I Wood, Senator for Queensland. The Labor Party's immigration policy is one of the most dangerous things that has ever been put before the Australian people.

What makes it more dangerous is the shrewd way Mr Whitlam is putting it before the public.

He says the Australian people would choose who would migrate to Australia.

This sounds very sweet until you analyse the situation.

By this he means that people living in Australia will nominate who they want to come to this country.

What most people will be thinking is that people of Australian or European birth would be doing the nominations.

The truth is that most of the nominations are coming from non-European people living in Australia. In fact, there were over 200,000 non-Europeans nominated to come to Australia last year, a very great proportion of the total nominations received.

The Labor Party has thrown overboard its White Australia policy, because of the influence of people like Premier Dunstan and others.

The people of Australia, by a great majority, would support Arthur Calwell in this matter in his opposition to the Labor Party's immigration policy.

No thinking person would want to import to Australia the problem which is worrying the USA and the United Kingdom.

The way would be open under Labor's policy for this to happen and if it did, it would be too late to put the clock back.

Letters, I Henning, Emeritus Professor. If the Government were returned at this election, not a few Australians, including myself, should be acutely distressed on one score at least; for it would presumably mean that a number of young men would be further detained in prisons here for having the courage to follow personal conscience and human dignity in resisting **military conscription**, and in all likelihood the coalition would proceed as if it had received a mandate to persist in its behaviour towards them.

The situation would be deplorable indeed, and one that our society can ill afford. Even if only as an act of national self-esteem, to justify and encourage a feeling that our outlook on life is not as fundamentally sick as the antics of our elected rulers often seem bent on making it appear, the Australian people owes it to itself not to miss this opportunity of righting an abysmal injustice.

Whatever the other issues in the election and however important some of them may be, they all give precedence to this moral one, which I like to think will be recognised by the electors throughout the country as over-riding.

Letters, C Puplick, State President, Young Liberal Movement. In his letter, Mr J McCarthy as President of the NSW Young Labor Association attempts to slander the Young

Liberal movement by alleging that we are in some way responsible for **the outbreaks of hooliganism** which have occurred at meetings of the Prime Minister.

This allegation is of course quite untrue, and I challenge Mr McCarthy to give one single instance of any Young Liberal acting in this manner. I am prepared to state quite categorically that Mr McCarthy will be unable to give a single instance of this sort of behaviour or indeed any scintilla of evidence to support his quite hysterical attempts to shift the blame, which rightfully belongs on the shoulders of the ALP, to other sources.

Letters, J Healey. A regrettable feature of present day democracy is the tendency of many people to **vote for policies which favour their own economic interests** rather than those of their under-privileged fellow citizens.

There is surely no place for this practice at present when, in this land of plenty, full employment is but a distant memory, housing is inadequate, pensioners try to eke out their scanty means, the Aborigines are among the world's most economically depressed people and there is a marked disparity between the educational standards of rich and poor schools.

Poverty is made, not by chance, but by man. Australia has the resources to provide all its citizens with a reasonable standard of living.

Yet the number of people living below or only marginally above the poverty line has been variously estimated as up to two million. The personal tragedies of those so affected can only be partially appreciated by the affluent sector of society.

The forthcoming Federal election will give us the opportunity to show if we are a caring Christian community.

We can demonstrate this by voting as we would if we lived in poverty or were likely to be among the 180,000 unemployed predicted for early next year by the Institute of Applied Economic and Social Research at Melbourne University.

Comment. You can see how disparate the views and interests of the electorate are. And, in passing, how scatter-brained some are in presenting them.

BALANCED, OBJECTIVE, COVERAGE

These are the final words from the *SMH* before the elections. It is generally thought that wavering voters take much notice of this Editor. In fact, many voters say they will not worry about the elections until they see his final words They will leave the election hubbub to others who know more about it. In the long run, they just vote as the *SMH* tells them.

Editorial, *SMH*. Mr Whitlam, in his final speech before the elections, said "Will you believe with me that Australia can be changed, should be changed, must be changed, if we are to have for ourselves and our children a better Australia, with a better grip on the realities of living in the modern world, and in our region as it really is? And will you believe with me that a new Government, a new program, a new team, is desperately needed to provide that change?" This, Mr Whitlam in the peroration of his policy statement. The rhetoric, even for a peroration, is extraordinarily empty. What are "the realities of living in the modern world"? And "our region as it really is" - what is that "really"? Above all, why precisely is there a "desperate need," other than Labor's natural hunger for power, for "a new Government, a new program, a new team"? Why "must" Australia be changed?

The truth is that Labor has been out of power for 23 years not because of gerrymanders or any other kind of sinister Government conspiracy. It has been out of power because it could not win trust widely enough among Australians.

What has changed in the Labor Party to make it suddenly more trustworthy now? The answer, so far as fundamental objectives are concerned, is nothing. And it is because nothing has changed - nothing more important than the substitution of fashionable catchcries about "the reality of living in the modern world" for the old discredited slogans of socialism -

that Labor has the gall to tell us that it is we who must change, Australia which "must be changed," to accommodate unchanging Labor.

Comment. Notice how **the language has got more inflammatory** as the campaigns have gone on.

Second Comment. I am surprised that a Paper, usually so balanced and avowedly determined to give everyone a fair go, has got right off the fence and came out swinging in favour of the Liberals. It will make people wonder about the "balance" that it gives to other matters.

In any case, the die is cast. Most electors have made up their minds. **The Libs or Labor?** You have only 24 hours to make up you mind. Will the ringing advice from the *SMH* sway the last swinging voters away from Labor?

Which way do you think it will all go?

DECEMBER NEWS ITEMS

Labor won Saturday's election by a country mile.... The result is that Labor will hold 68 seats in the House of Representatives....

The Liberals and Country Party will hold 45, and at the moment, 12 seats are in doubt....

If these seats are split equally, the final result will be 74 to 51.

Gough Whitlam became this nation's new Prime Minister, probably for four years.

Whitlam's first and immediate act was to **stop the draft of young men into the Military**. He also stopped the imminent arrest of draft evaders, and released all such men who are currently serving time in jail.

The new Minister for Industrial Relations will try to introduce four weeks annual leave for Public Servants. He also wants a shorter working week for them, and also extended maternity leave....

This is a nice pay-back to all those Public Servants who voted for Whitlam in the election. Whitlam also recognised China, and we exchanged Ambassadors. We are now catching up with most of the world after Nixon did the same thing.

Whitlam quickly made some decisions. One of these was to say that **racially selected sports teams from overseas cannot play against Australia.**

That means that **cricket and Rugby against South Africa are off the agenda**. The position with tennis and golf, which involve many other nations on occasions, is not yet clear.

Japan will set up two car manufacturing plants in Australia in the next years. Two companies, Toyota and Nissan will get permission....

Ford, Holden, Chrysler and Leyland will not be at all happy with this. It is after all, a pretty small market, now with **six majors competing locally**.

A boy in outback New Guinea was beheaded. Riots between two rival clans erupted. 60 men were injured. Police arrived to restore peace. They were met with a hail of arrows. Shotguns were fired over the head of the rioters, and this dispersed them.

The long-awaited first concert Sydney's Opera House was due to be held next Sunday to test the acoustics. The audience was to be Unionists of all sorts who had worked on the site. Their wives were also included. The total number exceeded the number of seats available....

So some workers were slotted in for a second performance. Those who missed out were unhappy. So a meeting was called, and the matter was not resolved....The outcome was that the second performance was cancelled for the moment, and **the first performance was delayed.**

1972 ACADEMY AWARDS

The French Connection	Gene Hackman
A Clockwork Orange	Malcolm McDowell
Fiddler on the Roof	Topol
The Last Picture Show	Timothy Bottoms, Jeff Bridges
Nicholas and Alexandra	Michael Joyston, Janet Suzman
Sunday Bloody Sunday	Peter Finch, Glenda Jackson
Klute	Donald Sutherland, Jane Fonda
The Hospital	George C Scott
McCabe and Mrs Miller	Warren Beatty, Julie Christie
Mary Queen of Scots	Vanessa Redgrave

BEST ACTOR   GENE HACKMAN

BEST ACTRESS   JANE FONDA

BEST MOVIE   FRENCH CONNECTION

1972 TOP OZ TUNES

Popcorn	Hot Butter
Puppy Love	Donny Osmond
Without You	Nilsson
American Pie	Don McLean
Imagine	John Lennon
Sylvia's Mother	Dr Hook
Cherish	David Cassidy
Brand New Key	Melanie
Rock 'n' Roll	Gary Glitter

Amazing Grace
Royal Scots Dragoon Guards

Daddy don't You Walk so Fast
Wayne Newton

The First Time Ever I Saw Your Face
Roberta Flack

Ernie (The Fastest Milman in the West)
Benny Hill

Most People I Know Think That I'm Crazy
The Aztecs

GIVE OUR POLITICIANS A BREAK

With the noise of the political battle still ringing in my ears, I would like to say a word pf sympathy for politicians of both Parties.

A politician's lot is not a happy one. I do not know what prompts a person to take on the role of politician. I know that there are some who do so out of "good" motives, and a lot who are rascals with motives that would generally be not considered as "good" at all.

I know it is accepted practice in Australia to denigrate politicians and their every action, and I find that most times I like to attack them myself.

But occasionally, like now, I think it proper to defend them. In this case, I refer to the terrible number of attacks they attract in just doing their jobs. I am not talking about abuse, quite personal abuse, that they and their families must bear. I am talking instead about the attacks that come from all sorts of writers who use the Press to castigate political opponents.

Let me illustrate this by talking about Gough Whitlam. He is more active than Bill MacMahon and therefore an easier target.

On a typical **day** at the end of November, I saw three separate attacks on him for his utterances in the *SMH*.

Firstly, at a public dinner, when it came to toasts, he mentioned that he preferred *Advance Australia Fair* to *God Save the Queen* as an anthem. **Very quickly, he is being admonished for his republicanism.**

Secondly, Abraham Lincoln was supportive of conscription of young men into the army for overseas fighting. Whitlam opposed that. One *SMH* Letter writer then charged that **Whitlam, on that evidence alone, was opposed to all the other virtues that Lincoln espoused.**

Thirdly, Whitlam said that he will offer Public Servants a wage increase and other benefits. A writer then argued that such a move will decrease the benefits that "real workers" will get, and castigates him for having this in his policy speech.

Comment. Here, I have no interest in whether the above three conclusions were true. The point I am making is that the writers based their Letters on negligible evidence, and complete lack of knowledge to pen their vindictive Letters.

Second comment. So I will stick my neck out a little against popular opinion and say that for all their faults, their human faults, they have a lot to put up with themselves.

SAVE THE DINGO

There are a lot of people in the frozen North of the world who are currently concerned about seals and the like. Various authorities with a spare abacus in hand have decided to count these creatures, and decided that their numbers have grown to the stage where they need culling.

So licences have been issued to shooters, and various boats have been put to sea so that quotas can be filled.

There has been outrage around the world at the thought of these cute little fellows being shot and killed, and lots of different protests invoked.

Over the last 50 years, we in Australia have seen cull licences issued to protect lots of species. And we have seen protestors do their best to stop the cull. The whales, the koalas, brumbies, kangaroos. All of these we have been urged to SAVE.

Back in 1972, we have an urger who wanted to save a different creature,

Letters, D Ford. If Cassidy's mob was successful in tracking down that Tasmanian tiger in Paddington perhaps Roger's next safari will be to search for a dingo at the Opera House - he is never likely to find the king of the Australian bushland in the bush!

Tourists are destined never to enjoy the sight or sound of this intelligent animal in its own habitat. At present they must be content to view the handsome dog miserably housed in an inadequate, small enclosure which is provided in most zoos and sanctuaries, etc. - the dingo pen at Kal Kari Wildlife Display warrants mention.

The dingo deserves a better deal - it has a rightful place in Australian ecology and for thousands of years it lived in harmony with the Aboriginal before the white settler took the land. It is time that the trusted custodians of our wildlife took steps to help upgrade the status of our active, native dog, and provided larger and more natural dingo enclosures.

The Melbourne Zoological Gardens at Royal Park has the famous, spacious lion enclosure. What a unique attraction it would be if Taronga, justly regarded as this nation's foremost zoo, established a landscaped paddock for, and worthy of, the exiled king of the Australian bush!

Comment. The dingo generally gets a bad Press in Australia. Worst of all, it is reputed to run into outback tents and steal babies. But here at least, it has one person who will give it a fair go.

WHAT TO BUY FOR CHRISTMAS

This is always a problem. This year, I have decided on presents for adults. **Especially for you.** I advise you to get in early though, because all sites say that stocks are limited, and will not last.

A Gift for Golfers! At Briacci and Brooks, amongst a fine collection of attractive "little" gifts for the man in your life, we came across the "Oneholer" Tie. It would make a superb gift for a golfing relative or friend who has the envied distinction of having holed-in-one. The tie is in fine crimpolene in maroon or navy with a silver motif, and it's exciting to know that it's the authentic international symbol of a hole-in-one, recognised throughout the world. Remember, you'll need Golf Club secretary's verification, so get it ready! The exclusive representatives of "Oneholer" trophies in Australia is Briacci and Brooks, The Men's Boutique, Double Bay.

Trendy Shoes and Handbags. When it comes to accessories, the young sophisticates head straight for Jose's of Double Bay. All the footwear that's top fashion is on display, including, of course, clogs and sandals in the most vogue-ish stylings. The smart fashion handbags make an-always-delightful Christmas gift that have been selected to match or contrast with the gorgeous shoes. In fact, we noticed particularly that there are elegantly youthful styles for all ages. Casual and leisure wear from top Australian makers and imports from all over the world are at realistic, down-to-earth prices! Illustrated is a platform sole and high heel, in white calf or black calf and satin. Jose, Goldman Lane.

George is Famous.... as the managing director of the Double Bay Pet Shop - we're told he gets a double ration of sunflower seed on Thursday night (after all, it's a hard day's night). George is a sulphur crested cockatoo who's "in" with the international set! But there's another reason to visit the pet shop - they've just received Red Factor canaries, which are usually impossible to get at Christmas time! They also have big cages, fish and aquarium equipment, the finest of imported and local pet accessories, veterinary lines, grooming aids, fresh meats and food for all pets. George is looking forward to chatting with you at the Double Bay Pet Shop.

Elegant Fashions and Gifts! Your columnist can never go by Adrienne's - the fashions and gifts in the windows positively lure one in! With holidays in the offing, we admired a bare-look gaily patterned dress by Go Gay. It's in washable cotton at only $25.50. Sketched is an irresistible glamour gown in black chiffon with a gorgeous rose at the neckline, $95 - other long dresses from around $40. Also, there are enchanting hand-embroidered gifts such as travel sachets with 2 compartments, $4.25; brush and comb sets, $3.25; covered coat hangers in vivid colours, $1.95; spectacle cases, jewel sachets, etc., at Adrienne's, The Bay Village, Double Bay.

A CHRISTMAS THOUGHT

Whether we like it or not, there will be Christmas again this year. That means lots of children screaming, lots of oldies meeting up for one occasion in the year, presents and pork, and greetings. I have lived through it many times, so I probably can do it again.

I have one brief thought that I will ramble on about. That is, what a lucky country we are, and have been, for most of my lengthy life. How lucky we are to have enough pelf and goods and houses and so on. We have enough that we can eat well, drink well, give presents without feeling pain, and lie round in houses that are getting better and better. There are some, a few, that cannot do this. But compare our position to many parts of the world, and we have lots to be contented with.

If we can spare a thought amid all the Christmas cheer to think and talk of this, it will be time well spent.

SUMMING UP 1972

I can point out several matters where there have been big improvements this year. **The first** is that the situation in Vietnam has improved. All of our troops have been removed, and now, under Whitlam no more will be sent. On top of that, conscription has gone, so that young men and their families will no longer live in dread as they approach 20 years of age. What a big relief.

The second is that peace in Vietnam is quite close. That too is a big relief, because that conflagration has kept the entire world on edge for about seven years. We all knew that if any of the big countries made a silly move, the world could have been plunged into a mighty war. Let us hope that one day very soon, diplomats in Paris and elsewhere will find a true peace.

A third matter is that the world has hardened its attitude to hijackers, and is now shooting and killing them. The threat posed by terrorists had kept growing until the world decided to take this action. Figures from future years show that this form of terrorism was reduced muchly from this time.

There have been other highlights. Nixon's fleeting efforts at diplomacy, decimalisation came and stayed, the Churches kept dying, and the dramas of the Olympic Games have brought terrorism into every house in the world. All sorts of smaller dramas kept us on our toes, but we were lucky enough to keep our heads down, and avoid many of the problems that countries overseas feel severely.

After all this, of course, 1972 marked the coming of Gough. For 23 years, this nation had been in the hands of a very measured and conservative Government. Labor had been in Opposition all that time, and had been held back by ideological leaders who had lost all contact with popular opinion.

Now, Gough has emerged, and looks like bringing change to every aspect of Australian life. He offers a brave new world, relief from the austerity of years of steady but stifling government, and a future full of shocks with a fair chance of being successful.

It's time that the nation had such a change. We should wish him well. But should also keep our fingers well and truly crossed.

COMMENTS FROM READERS

Tom Lynch, Spears Point…..Some history writers make the mistake of trying to boost their authority by including graphs and charts all over the place. You on the other hand get a much better effect by saying things like "he made a pile". Or "every one worked hours longer that they should have, and felt like death warmed up at the end of the shift." I have seen other writers waste two pages of statistics painting the same picture as you did in a few words….

Barry Marr, Adelaide….you know that I am being facetious when I say that I wish the war had gone on for years longer so that you would have written more books about it…

Edna College, Auburn…. A few times I stopped and sobbed as you brought memories of the postman delivering letters, and the dread that ordinary people felt as he neared. How you captured those feelings yet kept your coverage from becoming maudlin or bogged down is a wonder to me….

Betty Kelly. Every time you seem to be getting serious you throw in a phrase or memory that lightens up the mood. In particular, in the war when you were describing the terrible carnage of Russian troops, you ended with a ten line description of how aggrieved you felt and ended it with "apart from that, things are pretty good here". For me, it turned the unbearable into the bearable, and I went from feeling morbid and angry back to a normal human being….

Alan Davey, Brisbane….I particularly liked the light-hearted way you described the scenes at the airports as the American high-flying entertainers flew in. I had always seen the crowd behaviour as disgraceful, but your light-hearted description of it made me realise it was in fact harmless and just good fun….

MORE INFORMATION ON THESE BOOKS

Over the past 16 years the author, Ron Williams, has written this series of books that present a social history of Australia in the post-war period. They cover the period for 1939 to 1972, with one book for each year. Thus there are 34 books.

To capture the material for each book, the author, Ron Williams, worked his way through the *Sydney Morning Herald* and *The Age/Argu*s day-by-day, and picked out the best stories, ideas and trivia. He then wrote them up into 184 pages of a year-book.

He writes in a direct conversational style, he has avoided statistics and charts, and has produced easily-read material that is entertaining, and instructive, and charming.

They are invaluable as gifts for birthdays, Christmas, and anniversaries, and for the oldies who are hard to buy for.

These books are available at all major retailers. They are listed also in all leading catalogues, including Title Page and Dymocks and Booktopia.

****

THERE ARE 35 TITLES IN THIS SERIES
For the 35 years from 1939 to 1973

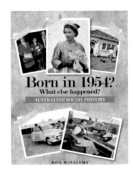

In 1954, Queen Elizabeth II was sent here victorious, and Petrov was our very own spy - what a thrill. Boys were being sentenced to life. Johnny Ray cried all the way to the bank. Church halls were being used for dirty dancing. Open the pubs after six? Were they ever closed?

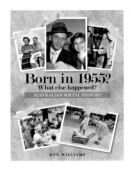

In 1955, be careful of the demon drink, get your brand new Salk injections, submit your design for the Sydney Opera house now, prime your gelignite for another Redex Trial, and stop your greyhounds killing cats. Princess Margaret shocked the Church, Huxley shocked the Bishops, and our Sundays are far from shocking.

****

Chrissi and birthday books for Mum and Dad and Aunt and Uncle and cousins and family and friends and work and everyone else.

Don't forget a good read and chuckle for yourself.

In 1956, the first big issue was the Suez crisis, which put our own Bob Menzies on the world stage, but he got no applause. TV was turned on in time for the Melbourne Olympics, Hungary was invaded and the Iron Curtain got a lot thicker. There was much concern about cruelty to sharks, and the horrors of country pubs persisted.

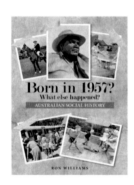

In 1957, Britain's Red Dean said Chinese Reds were OK. America avoided balance-of-payments problems by sending entertainers here. Sydney's Opera House will use lotteries to raise funds. The Russians launched Sputnik and a dog got a free ride. A bodkin crisis shook the nation.

****

AVAILABLE AT ALL GOOD BOOK STORES

AND NEWSAGENTS